Chelsfield

In From The Cold

Chelsfield

In From The Cold

A guided walk around Chelsfield
(or something like that)

Alan Cheesman

CELSFIELD

ISBN 978-0-9568957-0-7

Printed in Great Britain by the
MPG Books Group, Bodmin and King's Lynn

First published in the UK in 2011 by

Celsfield Press
5 Eton Road, Orpington, Kent BR6 9HD

For Janet

Contents

Front cover

Clockwise from top left: St Martin's, "Julian Brimstone", Cross Hall, and Well Hill looking north-east.

Back cover

The village from Court Road.

The Five Bells

Chelsfield Station and
Golden Arrow 1950

St Martin of Tours

Julian Brimstone
with pond 1935

White Hart (Bo Peep)
1890

Reasons To Be Cheerful

Introduction

Chelsfield is an area of much diversity in North West Kent consisting of a historic village, pleasant surrounding countryside and New Chelsfield, a 20th century development. It is in easy reach of London by both road and rail.

The name Chelsfield has had various spellings over the centuries and is derived from the Saxon Cile or Cels meaning cold and feld for field; therefore the name means Coldfield. It seems quite appropriate on a breezy winter's day while waiting for a bus delayed by the interminable road works which plague nearby Orpington but on a clear day at any time of the year there are some fine views to be had and old buildings of interest to be seen.

There is not thought to have been much in the way of habitation before the Saxon period although there could have been a small Anglo-Roman community. The usual flint arrow and axe heads have been found in small numbers together with some finds from the Roman period some of which can be seen at the Bromley Museum in Orpington. There were Roman villas at Orpington and Lullingstone, the remains of which are also available to view. It is thought that a Roman pottery may have existed at Pratts Bottom where a quantity of material, including floor and roof tiles, were found while foundations for a house in Stonehouse Road were being dug in 1928. The entry for Chelsfield in the Domesday Book gives the population as 20 villeins (villagers) and 4 smallholders who used 4 slaves. It has been estimated that the average size of a family at this time was five. If that was the case the villeins and smallholders would give the number of inhabitants of Chelsfield to be approximately 120 plus slaves. A mill is also mentioned. This would have to be a water mill for windmills were not introduced into this country until later and this mill may refer to a detached holding perhaps in the area now called St Mary Cray.

The Chelsfield parish area was once much larger and included Pratts Bottom, a good part of Green Street Green and a finger of land stretching down between Cudham and Knockholt as far as Cacketts Farm. This book is concerned with Chelsfield as it is accepted to be today plus Well Hill. Until 1934 Chelsfield Parish came under Bromley Rural District Council after which it then became part of the Orpington Borough. In 1965 this was swallowed by the cumbersome London Borough of Bromley.

Later we were told that London needed a second Mayor, although the reasons for this have never been completely explained as the first Mayor seemed to be doing a satisfactory job and putting on a jolly good show every year. In due course another was elected. The new Mayors, like some of the early owners of Chelsfield Manor have difficulty in recognising one end of their vast domain from the other, often referring to the inhabitants of Chelsfield and North East Kent in general as "Londoners".

Bromley is not good at preserving its heritage and as I write the former James Young coachworks in London Road is being torn down to be replaced with an over-sized hotel out of keeping with its surroundings. A look at Bromley centre will tell you that decades of piece-meal development have taken away much of the town's character and replaced it with a series of shopping precincts bolted together like Frankenstein's Monster along the length of the High Street. A new "part" is due to be fitted near Bromley South in the form of a hotel/cinema/restaurant complex described as a new "cultural heart" for the town. I always thought the heart went in the middle somewhere.

There are advantages to being on the fringe of this monolithic Borough, for as Bromley Limited has spent much time, effort and Council Tax on creating a consumer related disaster zone adjacent to the Civic Centre, outlying semi-rural districts like Chelsfield have remained relatively unscathed. Chelsfield has been lucky to have lost little of its heritage since the 1960's.

I first came to Chelsfield in the 1950's when my parents or grandparents would take me every few weeks from our home in Penge, now another Bromley backwater with which it only concerns itself when seeking to hive off parts of Crystal Palace Park for development, on the train from Penge East to Chelsfield, changing at Orpington. We would then walk along the path by the railway to Church Road where my aunts and uncle lived. It was always a good day out.

Many years later I moved to Orpington, very close to Chelsfield, and my interest in the area was rekindled. When I started leading walks for Environment Bromley (EnBro), which is independent of the Council, I began with Chelsfield before progressing to other, sometimes unlikely districts. I liked to be able to tell people a little about the places we were passing, for as Oliver Cromwell once said in one of his more enlightened moments " You see nothing if you don't know what you're looking at". Some suggested that I write a book about Chelsfield, I didn't think I had time, but eventually I decided to find it. So with no qualifications apart from being completely mad and a failed attempt at writing science fiction a long time ago, too embarrassing to recall, I set out to write one.

I mentioned my project to Geoffrey Copus who was most helpful and encouraging and did not seem to mind that I had hi-jacked most of his book in order to knock out; I mean compile, this work. Anne Blatcher of St. Martin's kindly looked over my section on the church and presented me with a long list of mistakes to correct. Philip Lane took time off from photographing top models (of trains) to add his local knowledge. I would also like to thank John Barnes for providing useful information on St Martin's bells.

This guide is in the form of a walk which some of you may be able to complete in a day but I think best done in two or more stages giving you time to observe your surroundings thoroughly. I have given information on transport links where they exist but they may be subject to change as may be places of refreshment. The maps are not to scale. I have included a lot of historical background best read before you walk as reading and walking at the same time can cause accidents. As well as the main walk I have included four additional walks, not essential for historical content, but they ensure complete coverage of the Chelsfield area. I have made every attempt to ensure accuracy in all the information given but some smart a...alec is bound to find something they consider wrong and if that is the case the error will be mine alone and no one else can be blamed.

It can be difficult to date some buildings especially if they have had recent work and on occasions I have been very approximate. Looking at some "restored" buildings reminds me of the story of a man exhibiting a veteran car at a show. A visitor approaches and says, "That's a nice car, did you restore it yourself?"

Owner; "Yes indeed, as a matter of fact I dug it up in my garden."

Visitor; "Well I never. What was it like?"

Owner; "It was just a frame, no mechanical or body parts."

Visitor; "So you built it up from the chassis?"

Owner; "Not really, it was rotten, all I could salvage was a spring-hanger bolt."

Visitor; "You mean to tell me the only original part of this car is a spring-hanger bolt?"

Owner; "Well actually no, it broke last week and I had to fit a new one."

Fortunately none of the important buildings in Chelsfield are like this but there are one or two dubious examples.

The title of the book is an obvious play on the name Chelsfield. Until now there has been no guide to the area while most places around have had one or something like it. Books on Kent give Chelsfield little attention and often the cold shoulder. As this is something like a guide to Chelsfield, it comes in from the cold. As for the title of this section; as I write Ian Drury is singing "Reasons To Be Cheerful" on the radio and now I have completed the introduction which I have written last, as you do, and enjoyed every minute of it, this heading seems appropriate.

Chelsfield Station from the coal yard in the 1960s showing the old station buildings.
(Philip Lane collection)

Another view from the coal yard showing the footbridge to the residential streets.
The lorry is probably an ex-military Bedford. (Philip Lane collection)

Class F 4-4-0 locomotive enters Chelsfield with a train from the direction of Sevenoaks passing the points to the goods yard. (Philip Lane collection)

Kirtley ex-LCDR 0-4-4 class R engine, built 1891. This and similar types of small tank were the mainstay of Southern local services. Orpington-Sevenoaks shuttle is shown c1925.

Chelsfield Station today. Apart from the railway infrastructure the view
has not changed much since 1868.

The author at Chelsfield Station. Two previous
arrivals here later became famous writers,
so I thought...

From Chelsfield Station To World's End

A walk of about 1½ miles with ¼ mile to transport at the end
(Mon to Sat)

We will begin our look at Chelsfield at the place many have arrived, particularly before the growth of motor transport; Chelsfield Station. You can arrive here by train from Orpington or Sevenoaks or on bus R1. Parking can be difficult during week days. Toilets on the station are usually open a.m.

The line was built for The South Eastern Railway as a shorter route to Sevenoaks than that already existing via Swanley. It was authorised on the 30th August 1862. Work began in 1863 with Jay as contractors and engineer Brady. Jay tendered £600,000 for St John's to Tonbridge; but someone got their sums wrong and Jay was bankrupt in about a year; their assets were seized by the receiver who allowed work to continue under his supervision. Most workers were based at Tubs Hill near Sevenoaks but railway huts were also situated next to Warren Road Chelsfield and near to where Knockholt Station now stands. 1,500 men were employed at one time with five contractors' locomotives, sixteen pumping and winding engines, five hundred earth wagons and a hundred and fifty horses.

The line to Chislehurst opened in 1865 but engineering problems delayed the remainder. Experimental goods trains were run through our area on the 28th February 1868, passenger traffic ran to Sevenoaks on the 3rd of March and to Tonbridge on the 1st May.

The Railway did not initially plan a station at Chelsfield because there was not much near the route to stop for, but William Waring, Lord of the Manors of Chelsfield and Hewitts, wanted a station conveniently placed to convey his goods and as the Company needed his land, it came to pass that Chelsfield Station opened with the line.

Apart from the platforms here now the original station had a carriage siding on the north east side and a three track goods yard in the areas now occupied by the car park. There were weatherboard railway cottages and a "Station House" where there is now a modern town house development. A footbridge was not constructed over the goods yard until 1926. The north east siding track was lifted just before the line was electrified in 1935; an electricity supply station now stands here. Electric services began on the 6th of January.

On the 4th of November 1940, at 7.20 p.m., enemy action brought down the footbridge over the main lines onto the first coach of an e.m.u. (electric train). One person was killed and six slightly injured. The bridge was rebuilt to the same standard design in 1941. There are rumours that this may be replaced again soon. The goods yard was closed on the 18th of April 1964. The signal box at the south end of the down platform was destroyed by fire on the 13th of May 1971 and not replaced. The station building itself was burnt down in 1976, probably due to an electrical fault and was replaced by a contemporary design seen here today. It is a "System 70" building with a centrally positioned booking office from which the whole station can be supervised.

Famous writers connected with Chelsfield Station

Edith Nesbit came here when she was living with her mother and two brothers at Halstead village, between 1872 and 1875 when she was aged 14 to 17. Three years may not seem very long you might think, but these were the most formative years of her life. This period was the first she had known in a typical family home in her native England since her very early years. She was born in Kennington, South London in 1858 to Sarah and John Collis Nesbit. When Edith, or Daisy, as everyone called her, was just approaching her fourth birthday, her father died at a friend's house. He left home one day and never returned. At her young age she could not understand why. This loss was to prey on her mind for years, if not the rest of her life. Many of her stories end with the emotional return of one or more parents, not least father's return at the end of "The Railway Children". "My daddy, oh my daddy".

Her father's death threw more responsibility onto her mother and the children were looked after by a nurse. In 1866 Edith's elder sister Mary developed consumption. For the next four years, on doctors advice, Sarah Nesbit took her family from place to place around Europe attempting to make her ailing daughter's life more comfortable. Edith was rarely happy on these travels. After Mary died in 1871 Mrs Nesbit sought a home in Kent, the county she loved and chose Halstead Hall which she rented from Mrs Louisa Man.

Edith and her brothers, Harry and Alfred, two and four years older respectively, were fascinated by the railway and spent many hours playing games on and around the track and station, which, due to the lack of "health and safety" fencing in those days, were easy to access. Railway staff, and one may have been the model for Perks the porter, were unlikely to have shown much concern about the activities of the children, or teenagers as we would call them today, as youngsters at that time had the sense to move away from an oncoming train and not stand in front of it.

In later years a fellow writer, journalist and historian Oswald Barron, with whom Edith had collaborated, encouraged her to use childhood reminiscences to construct stories. The first book of these stories, "The Story of the Treasureseekers" was published in 1899. "The Railway Children" first saw the light of day in serial form in "The London Magazine" in 1905 and appeared in book form in 1906. It became E. Nesbit's greatest hit and is still in the best selling children's book chart today; the equally successful film is shown on T.V. at least every Christmas and in 2010 was even the subject of a play performed at Waterloo with a real steam engine. Edith's success was that she had lived out the adventures she wrote about.

On the 2nd of March 1921 another future writer came to Chelsfield, at the age of seven with her mother from Hither Green. Miss Read (Dora Shafe, or Saint, after her marriage), writes in her book "Early Days" of her arrival at Chelsfield Station:——

"........I stood dumbfounded.

There was no one on the platform except for the guard of the train. I had never seen a station like this. There were no posters, no trolleys, no litter bins, no milk churns! Furthermore, once the train had pulled away everything was still and quiet.

Before me, on a green bank, sheltered from the wind, primroses were growing, and somewhere high above, birds were singing, which I learnt soon after were skylarks, indigenous to this chalky North Downs country!"

There may not be so many skylarks now but it can still seem as peaceful in between trains.

Miss Read became a teacher but did not begin writing until after World War 11, starting with light essays for "Punch" and other journals. She then wrote on educational and country matters and worked for the B.B.C. She married another teacher and had one daughter. She was awarded the M.B.E. in 1998 for services to literature. She is best known for her novels of village and English rural life. The first of these "Village School" was published in 1955. She continued to write about the fictitious villages of Fairacre and Thrush Green until her retirement in 1996 when she was living in Berkshire.

Walk up Station Approach towards Windsor Drive and turn sharp left down the drive to Station Cottages. These are one of several pairs built for Waring estate workers c.1860. It may have been convenient to have labourers living close to their work here. This pair has been extended but retain their period charm.

Walk back past the station building to the steps next to the car park entrance and up to the footpath which runs parallel to the tracks. Another view of Station Cottages can be obtained from here if not obscured by foliage in the summer months. You pass the end of The Woodlands on the edge of Chelsfield Park and the footpath becomes a bridleway. On the right hand side was Oxenden Wood. Some of the trees still stand in the gardens of houses which now back onto the path.

Soon we come to a disused bridge over the railway, built for agricultural usage when the land on both sides of the line was in the same ownership. A dirt track came here from Court Lodge Farm and perhaps goods and livestock were taken to and from the station this way. Although no longer used, the bridge shows signs of recent repair work.

As we pass the end of The Meadows there is a large new house (2009/2010) with an outbuilding/garage that resembles a chapel. This is the type of house now being built in this area.

Chelsfield Park

The development of Chelsfield Park began in 1921. You could either buy one of a small selection of homes by Homesteads architect Hubert V. C. Curtis of the Strand or purchase a plot available from £100 (£10 down and 5d a day!) and build your own. Development has continued to this day with infilling and some redevelopment. There are some impressive houses. New legislation to ban garden infilling may help retain some of the green but could also lead to a more rapid demolition of older houses.

If you are interested in the architecture of the last ninety years or so you might enjoy a stroll around these roads. Within the Chelsfield Parish, Chelsfield Park consists of Homestead Road, Julian Road, The Meadows and The Woodlands with parts of Chelsfield Hill, Church Road, Meadway and Worlds End Lane. The Park actually extends to Sevenoaks Road at Pratts Bottom.

There is not room to describe everything; and in any case, appreciation is in the mind of the beholder; but some of the properties that caught my eye while walking around are mentioned in the following:——

Opposite Julian Road and in Worlds End lane is a terrace of three small Edwardian houses which for practical purposes marks the end of the Green Street Green section of this road. The part of the Lane between Julian Road and Homestead Road is still semi-rural and maybe looks similar to as it would in the 20's. Number 120 is probably one of the first built here on a large plot. In Chelsfield Park mock Tudor seems to predominate among the newer houses, as many have the ambition to live in a fake Tudor dwelling, but if you are going to build them you might as well do it properly and those at 181 "Woodcroft" and 181A are fine examples with some interesting features; 187A is a modernist house in angular style; 150 has a double porch in art deco style; 168 is a modern residence with impressive frontage and Georgian style windows; 215 is an example 1930's mock Tudor; 221 (1949) has attractive rustic style timber boarding to the upper floor; 231 is a 20's weatherboard bungalow and 188, "Cedar Cottage" is a larger probably 30's house.

In Homestead Road number1 is a large new house (2009/2010) in Victorian style; 8 a modern House with perhaps some Georgian influence; 9 another good mock Tudor and 24 is in Palladium mansion style with huge Ionic pillars, looking a bit like "Graceland". There can be no doubt that Elvis would have loved Chelsfield. By contrast opposite is 21, a nice 30's bungalow with the entrance at the inner angle of the frontage typical of the period and next door 23, probably late 40's with rustic weather boarding. Well known local photographer Phillip Lane lives in this road and has a vast collection of archive material of Chelsfield and surrounding areas. He has also put much effort into the construction of a landscaped model railway in his garden and has open days, currently three a year, on which children young and old can go and enjoy the trains.

In The Woodlands, which together with The Meadows was laid out in 1929, number 8 is an attractive Kentish weatherboard cottage. In Meadway 17 and 19 are a nice complementary pair of 20's style houses although of later construction. The Meadows includes some pleasing homes including modern buildings at numbers 2 and 6 with portico entrance porches (c2007), 16, is1930's and tile-hung and 21, a modern house with wide tile-hung frontage. Julian Road contains mostly modest size houses and bungalows from the 20's on.

Oxenden Wood Road has more attractive homes including 33 which is a typical 1930's Chelsfield Park house enlarged more recently and 53, a nicely maintained smaller example. A private drive serves The Chelsfield Park Recreation and Sports Club, formed in 1930 when a cricket pitch, tennis court and pavilion were created. After World War 11 they were renovated in association with Green Street Green Cricket Club and the ground was purchased by the Residents Association in 1950.

Off Worlds End Lane, to the west of the junction with Oxenden Wood Road is a footpath known as "squirrels path" which goes down through Chelsfield Hill Wood to Sevenoaks Road. About half way down is an open space where a good view can be obtained across Pratts Bottom.

Along the bridleway beside the railway we see the cutting deepen towards the entrance to Chelsfield Tunnel, 597 yards long (about 547 metres), which takes the line under Chelsfield Downs. Did Edith and her brothers walk through this tunnel? In "The Railway Children" the paper chase goes through a tunnel and the children rescue a straggler who has fallen and injured himself. The author gives a good description of the tunnel's interior, so Chelsfield Tunnel may be where she obtained her knowledge. Trains were less frequent in those days, the times well known and usually kept to! If a train did approach there are alcoves in which they could take cover.

The line climbs between Chelsfield and Knockholt with a gradient of 1 in 118 to 1 in 170 and "Schools" class steam locomotives hauling express trains would slow from 60 m. p. h. to just over 50 m.p.h. in this distance.

As we walk on, we pass, on the right, the site of World's End Farm. How it got it's name is uncertain; it may have been thought a long way from the village or could have been on a boundary. The first recorded use of the name was in 1730. The original name in the Manorial records was Newfield. The farmhouse was demolished in 1962 and Brimstone Close, with access from Worlds End Lane, was built by Sanderson Brothers builders of Chelsfield village. On the left of the bridleway is Chelsfield Riding School, established here for over fifty years.

We emerge into Church Road. Turn right and pass the end of Worlds End Lane into Chelsfield Hill. A bungalow situated between "Hawthorns" and "Fircroft" is called "Bramleigh" but currently carries no name. Miss Read lived at "Bramleigh" although she refers to it in her book as a house, one of the first homes on the Chelsfield Park estate (possibly the first), just at the top of the hill which leads down to Pratts Bottom. She lived here with her parents and elder sister from 1921 when the home was new, attending the village school to which she would walk once or twice a day, although sometimes she would cadge a lift on a tradesman's wagon, something no child would dream of doing now.

Miss Read wrote in "Early Days":—

"At Chelsfield I came into my own and have never ceased to be thankful".

She may not be the only one.

Opposite the house was a pond where she and her friends would fish for tadpoles. The story goes that it was filled in after a woman's body was found in it.

Also at the top of the hill was a notice instructing drivers of horse drawn vehicles to engage the skid pan. The pan or drag-shoe was shaped like a deep narrow handle-less coal shovel which was attached to the cart by a stout chain. It was placed under the rear near-side wheel in such a way as to prevent it from turning. The vehicle was then moved on with the wheel locked and ploughing a furrow in the road until level ground was reached again when the cart stopped and backed out of the drag. Wagoners had long thought the fitting of brakes to carts was "cissy", more suitable for gentlemen's carriages.

The next house is "Fircroft", built in the 1980's in the style of a 20's house, and then "Southover", c 1934, and home of architect Grorge A. Rose who designed this building and also the village hall. Roseneath Close, on the site of a house of the same name, is the extent of the Chelsfield Parish. No. 1 became the home of broadcaster Brian Matthews. He had a small theatre built onto the house for private use where plays were performed.

If you choose to leave the walk here the nearest transport is at Pratts Bottom where infrequent bus services, 402, R5 and R10 can be found except on Sundays. Alternatively return to Chelsfield Station via the bridleway, or using the map choose a route through Chelsfield Park.

Chelsfield Station to World's End

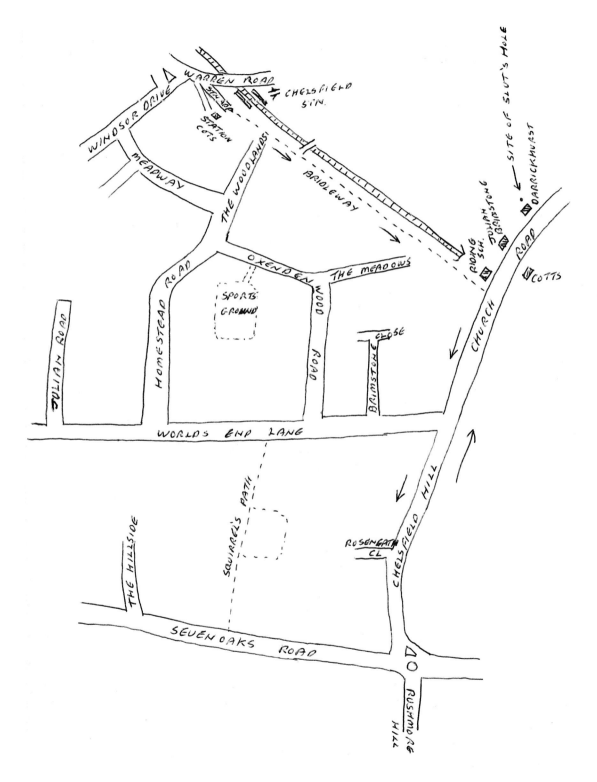

A neat looking house in The Woodlands.

Elvis would have liked this house in Homestead Road.

"Bramleigh", Miss Read's former home and probably the first building in Homestead's Chelsfield Park, looking original apart from replacement windows and missing chimney pot.

This deteriorating gate in Church Road I think marks the site of the civil defence post in both World Wars.

World War I Special Constables guarding the railway tunnel. (Geoffrey Copus collection)

Hewitts Farm Cottages from the footpath which runs to the east of the farmhouse.
As it is one of the few paths not on the walk, here is a picture of it.

"Julian Brimstone Cottages" from the golf course showing a number of later additions.

The ancient "Julian Brimstone" farmhouse.

"Darrickhurst", once several cottages. "Slutt's Hole" well was adjacent.

"Linden Cottage" c1960.

Clearing the garden, early 50's; Bert and a helper.

Me, good looking even then, on one of the rare occasions when I made myself useful.

Alice, left, and Win Head.

Bert and Alma Head.

Chelsfield Downs

A walk of about 2½ miles with ¼ mile from transport at the beginning

If you are beginning this section of the walk here the buses mentioned at the end of the last section stop near the roundabout at the junction of Sevenoaks Road and Rushmore Hill. Then it is a short but steep walk to the top of Chelsfield Hill. Continuing in the direction of Chelsfield village at various places you can access Chelsfield Lakes Golf Course, formerly Chelsfield Downs G. C, and walk parallel to the road without having to watch out for traffic. The course covers a large part of the Downs but the lakes are more like large ponds. It is a public course but please remember to use the paths where possible and keep out of the way of the golfers and their balls!

In both World Wars a civil defence post was established here near the highest point; I believe about where there is still an old farm gate, not far from opposite the end of Worlds End Lane. Special Constables would be stationed here and be on the lookout for enemy agents who might want to sabotage the railway tunnel or think this area a good place to parachute into. It is not recorded if any spies were caught.

On the right of Church Road are a pair of cottages, built in 1878 on the site of earlier dwellings. They are the "Julian Brimstone Cottages", although one is now called "Key Largo". The architect was George St. Pierre Harris whose best known local work is Aynscombe Angle in Orpington. He set up as an architect in 1876 so this was one of his earlier commissions.

Opposite is the "Julian Brimstone" former farmhouse, until about 1920 known as "Gillmans Brimstone". It is 17th cent. or earlier, refaced with red brick on the ground floor and tile hung above. It is thought that the name may have originated with John Brim, who was living in Chelsfield in 1301, as Brim's Tone or Brim's Farm. The origin of Gillmans is unknown. The Petley family acquired the farm in the 15th cent. and retained it until 1806 when it was sold to John Fuller, at that time living at Hewitts.

The farmhouse and 219 acres were sold in 1920 to Homesteads Limited, originally William Carter's Estates which adopted their new name in 1903. It cost them £ 8,000. Building began on south west side of the railway in 1921. Homesteads manager Percy Curtis lived in the farmhouse and sold from here. It was at this time the name Julian appeared and I think it likely it was after a member of the Curtis family. Next to the house stands a stone and brick barn.

Miss Read would often walk to school with children from the cottages. She remembered honeysuckle on the walls and sometimes being attacked by geese which were resident on a pond which was between the "Brimstone" farmhouse and "Darrickhurst". Today you are more in danger from drivers who can't tell the difference between a country road and a motorway. " Darrickhurst," formerly several cottages of the 18th cent., is brick with flint additions. There used to be a well , now filled in, close to the rear of the building, which went by the intriguing name of "Sluts's Hole". Disappointingly it was probably just a corruption of "sluice". By 1919 it was being referred to as "Stutts Hole".

Further along Church Road we come to an originally latter half of the 19th cent. pair of cottages on the left. They are "Linden Cottage "and "Codlin Cottage". Linden Cottage used to be 2 Codlin Cottages but members of my family were responsible for re-naming it. This is where my uncle and aunts lived, Herbert (Bert) Head, his wife Alma and Alice and Winifred (Win) Head (cousins). Alma had become an invalid by the time I knew her. Bert worked hard all his life mainly on farms, including Broke Farm for Henry May. He could turn his hand to anything ; he improved the cottage and built an extension, and used a good part of the garden to grow fruit and vegetables. This still left a large area of woodland stretching down to the fields below. He had a large market garden tractor controlled by handle-bars with the operator walking behind. He would not let anyone else use it in case they killed themselves. I remember the cottage had a large cellar, used for storage and home brew, which may form the basement of the current building.

After Alma died, and after a respectful period Bert married Alice. Sadly this marriage was short lived. Shortly before he was due to retire from his last job with the National Trust at Knole, Bert arrived home in his old Standard 10, which he maintained himself, and suffered a heart attack as, or just after, he drove in at the bottom of the garden. After this, I think in 1969, the two remaining aunts decided to move away. "Linden Cottage" has been almost completely rebuilt and enlarged but its neighbour, although also enlarged still shows weatherboard on its east facing wall. These may well have been the "clapboarded" cottages where Miss Read remembers Hilda's grandmother living.

Jack Cade Rebellion

John Petley and John Jeter of Chelsfield participated in the Jack Cade Rebellion of 1450. Citizens of Henry V1 suffered from corrupt and incompetent government (how different things are today?). He had lost the land in France that his father had captured at great effort, lost control of the Channel so the French could take delight in raiding the English coast, and of course taxes were high. The King was happy to let the Duke of Suffolk take the blame and had him exiled to the continent. On the way the ship was intercepted by Kentish sailors and the Duke executed; his headless body washed up on the coast. The Lord Lieutenant of Kent, Lord Saye and Sele, treasurer of England, threatened to turn the whole county into a Royal deer park.

Jack Cade, who was Irish and claimed to be John Mortimer and cousin of the Duke of York, lived in Sussex but happened to be in Ashford at the beginning of the Rebellion and took command of it. The rebels, who at one time numbered 20,000 met at Blackheath in June. After marching though Farnborough to Sevenoaks, and probably past the bottom of what is now Chelsfield Hill, they ambushed a contingent of the King's men in woods at the "Battle of Solefields" killing 26.

There is a plaque at the site today at the junction of Solefields Road and Tonbridge Road at Sevenoaks. The rebels then marched on London while the King fled to Kenilworth. After executing Saye and Sele and his son Crowmer, Sheriff of Kent, the rebels were stopped by an army raised by the Mayor. The following day the Lord Chancellor accompanied by the Archbishop of Canterbury accepted the rebels' petition and granted a pardon.

Despite a general pardon 49 of Cade's followers were executed and Cade hunted down. The place of his apprehension is disputed between Cade Street near Heathfield and Iden Green near Benenden; (on balance I think Heathfield is more likely). It is known for certain that it was the 13th of July 1450. The story goes that Sir Richard Walker, now Sheriff of Kent with Alexander Iden and others found Cade playing bowls. Not unreasonably Cade was not ready to come quietly, put up a fight, was wounded by Iden and died soon afterwards.

Cade's body was dragged through the streets of London. His head was placed on a spike on London Bridge and his quarters sent, after being part boiled to preserve them, to towns across the country for display as a warning to others. One piece was reportedly stolen by supporters from the town gate to which it was affixed.

Now we move on and the next property we come to is "Pecks Cottage", now one home it was built in c1850 as a pair of cottages on the site of Pax farmhouse. One of the first tenants was Stephen Kimber. One of the original pair was let to him in 1858 at 8s 9d per month, including rates, taxes and repairs. When Stephen died in 1884 Mr Waring let his widow and children stay on at the same rent. She died in 1923 just short of her 100th birthday.

From here you can continue along Church Road to the church and village, but my devious walk will take you along footpath 258 which runs about 45 degrees back towards Pratts Bottom. On the map this is a straight line but is not quite that simple and to try and save you the trouble of searching for the exit at the other end I will give you additional directions. Walk through the cottage garden and the gap in the hedge, bear slightly left and walk between the rows of fruit trees. Then go to the left of the pond. Walk towards and pass an electricity pylon, a footpath marker and 18th tee. Go along the surfaced golfers' path for a short distance to a clump of bushes, pass to the left of these and follow the mown path down the hill bearing slightly left at tee 4. From here you get an excellent view over Pratts Bottom, once part of old Chelsfield .

You emerge from the path onto Sevenoaks Road, opposite Stonehouse Road, named after a farm of the same name. Sevenoaks Road was constructed in 1832, through the land of Alderman Atkins of Halstead, to bypass Rushmore Hill and Star Hill which coaches found hard going .A bus stop is a short distance to the right of the footpath where the 402 stops Monday to Saturday, but this is an hourly service so check the timetable if you intend to use it. It is not too long a walk to Pratts Bottom from here should you wish to visit.

Cross Sevenoaks Road at the traffic island, turn left and after passing a couple of 30's detached houses you have green on both sides. Keep to this side of the road when you reach London Road. There is a group of mid 20th cent. houses on this corner. Turning the corner you enter Broke Bottom; the name coming from broke or brook which is thought to have flowed here.

On weekdays you will know you are approaching Knockholt Station by the commuter cars parked on the side of the road. You pass the entrance to Broke Hill Golf Club, formerly Broke Farm, first recorded in 1731. In 1934 a proposal to build 1820 houses was made, reduced to 600 the next year. Only a few were built before the war and town and country planning restraints intervened. The original farmhouse was demolished in the late 60's by Cadbury Schweppes Pension Fund, which had become the owner and operations merged with Hewitts. In 1992 the golf course opened with a club house on approximately the same site as the farmhouse. What looks like a group of farm buildings next to the road is in fact a later residential development. A gate adjacent to this is the entrance to a footpath across the golf course to Halstead.

The trains at Knockholt are as at Chelsfield and the 402 bus stops here. This station is within Chelsfield Parish; the boundary running around it.

After the opening of Chelsfield Station there was considerable disgruntlement about its position particularly among farmers, most of whom found the journey with their goods quite arduous, through the village and along Warren Road, sometimes called "Long Warren". Eventually £2,000 was raised by the farmers to build another station on land purchased from Mr. Waring. Work began in 1872 and this station opened on the 1st May 1876, named Halstead or "Halstead for Knockholt". In 1900 a gentleman sent a parcel to Halstead in Essex which ended up here. The gentleman had some influence with the S.E.R. and in October 1900 the station name changed to Knockholt or "Knockholt for Badger's Mount".

Edith Nesbit and her brothers were able to watch the ground work for the station's construction which included the removal of large quantities of chalk which the railway company were afterwards able to sell. Quarrying continued for sometime after and in 1898 the Railway bought more land, again from Mr. Waring to extend the quarry area. The Lord of the Manor appears to have done exceedingly well out of the line. The quarry was re-opened in March 1953 to supply material for sea defences following the North Kent floods of that year.

Edith Nesbit may have developed her liking for quarries here as she mentions such sites in some of her books. In "Five Children and It" the house is near a chalk quarry and the gravel pit where the children find the "Psammead ", or sand fairy, although the quarry here is thought to be based on one near Rochester.

Edith came back to see her old home several times. She brought Hubert Bland before their marriage and in later years she was accompanied by others such as Bower March. Their journeys would be via Halstead/Knockholt Station The station was mentioned in some of her stories; called "Knockholt Junction" in one.

The original station buildings were of timber (the main building burnt down in 1981) and have all been replaced apart from the canopy on the down platform with its curved roof but without the fancy boarding it once had. The goods yard was closed in 1965. There was a signal box on the down platform at the London end where the platform narrows. The box, called "Wheatsheaf" was closed on 1st August 1973. An iron footbridge was replaced by the concrete one about 1970. The quarry site is bisected by a modern road bridge carrying the A21. You will find a Victorian post box in a brick post near the booking office.

Sir Waldron Smithers M. P. represented first Chislehurst and then (due to boundary changes) Orpington from 1924 until his death in 1954. When Parliament was sitting he could be seen on the platform at Knockholt waiting for the express train to Cannon Street which he is said to have had arranged to stop here for him at 9.04 a.m. A railway time-table for 1930 shows no less than seven trains stopping at Knockholt between 9a.m. and 10a.m., all to Cannon Street and only one stopping at Chelsfield. By the 1950's the situation had changed and it may have taken some pressure from the M.P. to retain his transport. When Sir Waldron died one contender for the seat was Margaret Thatcher but she was rejected by the local party who apparently wanted a male candidate. (History could have been very different here).

Mr John Bowen of nearby Wheatsheaf Farm began a timber business in 1846. At first household fuel was sold, but by the time the railway came Bowen and his son Percival were conducting an international trade, exporting local timber and importing exotic wood from abroad. Wood was loaded and unloaded from wagons at the station goods yard where there was a five ton capacity crane. They continued to sell firelighters which went by the names of "pimps", small bundles of twigs, and "bavins", bundles of brushwood for use in larger ovens. The firm held a Royal Warrant to supply firelighters to Buckingham Palace between 1905 and 1965, obtained through the influence of Sir William Hart-Dyke of Lullingstone. The business closed in 1965. If you wish to see Wheatsheaf Farmhouse it is about a quarter of a mile further down London Road and just around the corner in Wheatsheaf Hill; two storied with neat wooden porch; mid 19th cent in appearance but has older origins. You would never believe that it had once been the centre of a hive of industry.

On leaving the station you pass the late Victorian "Station House" and take the by-way which leads across the railway and then the A21. On reaching the south-eastern corner of Chelsfield Lakes G.C. keep right to the hedge until you reach a footpath sign and then bear left in its general direction up the slope and over to find the exit onto the southern end of Court Road, the Orpington Bypass; A224. It was constructed between 1924 and 1928 by Fordyce Bros. to relieve Orpington centre. Its effect on Chelsfield was to separate the village centre from the church and spell the eventual demise of the village as a shopping centre. It surely would have been possible to run the new road to the south west of the church without increasing the cost by too much but apparently the main objectors to this route were a certain wealthy family and money counts. This part of the bypass was named Court Road in 1932. Things could have been worse if a proposed Dartford Crossing approach road had been put though Chelsfield.

In 1986 a proposal for a shopping and leisure complex was submitted. It involved 1 million square feet of retail space, 165,000 square feet of leisure space, parking for 6,000 cars, a coach park and a 10 screen cinema. This scheme would have proved devastating for the area and there was widespread opposition to the plan, so vociferous that even those in authority who normally turned a deaf ear to such protests could not do so and the proposal was rejected on appeal in 1988.

About half a mile north up the bypass are the main entrances to Hewitts Farm and Chelsfield

Lakes Golf Centre. Hewitts Farm shop sells local produce and honey made from local sources, some with extra local pollen, said to be good for hay-fever sufferers, but I can't offer any guarantees. Also in the yard is Fired Earth Aga Shop, kitchen and bathroom specialists. Apart from the usual golfing facilities the Golf Centre has a bar and licensed restaurant; not cheap but not unreasonable either considering the type of establishment. It also caters for functions.

From where you left the golf course carefully cross the bypass to a footpath on the far side slightly to the right. The path should go straight across the field, part of Hewitts Farm, but in practice you follow the track around and look for a way through the crop to the sign on the opposite side between a modern pair of Hewitts Farm Cottages and the industrial building. The latter called "Orchard Building" is occupied by Soundcraft who make doors, windows, staircases and other items of timber building materials.

Turn left into Hewitts Road. Soon you come to Hewitts Farmhouse; 18th cent., two stories plus attic, the normal layout for a Kentish farmhouse of the period.

Hewitts

Hewitts is said to have been named after Jeffery de Hewat (spelling approximate) who came into possession of the Manor during the reign of Henry VIII, but it appears to be the other way around. Hewitt means "cutting place where a clearing has been made in woodland", (Hiewet, Hewette in 1268). William Petley acquired the Manor in 1522. William also owned property in Beddington, Bromley, Cudham, Knockholt, Lewisham and Otford. On his death he was succeeded by his son Stephen who built a new house on the site in Halstead which was later to become Halstead Place.

The Petley family who had been living in Downe from the 13th cent., or perhaps before have an interesting history, apart from the afore mentioned involvement in the Cade Rebellion. In 1602 a William Petley was convicted of the homicide of Samuel Renolds of Maidstone by stabbing him in the chest at the Bull at Otford. Convicted at Dartford Assizes in February he managed to "get off" by "pleading clergy", meaning he could read and write and was able to escape punishment. It seems that then as now if you are rich or famous there is often a way of getting lenient treatment. Brothers Robert and Anthony Petley were Royalist sympathizers at the time of the Commonwealth and were under suspicion.

On the death of Thomas Petley in 1664 the family fortunes began to slide. About 100 acres of Hewitts was sold. Ralph Petley of Riverhead inherited the remaining land on his father's death in 1751 while the Chelsfield properties went to Charles Petley, an ordnance storekeeper at Chatham, Upon his death in 1765 his wife Elizabeth took charge of the estate. In 1781 the farmhouse and some surrounding land was sold to John Fuller.

John Fuller prospered and built himself a new house called "Woodlands" near the village, into which he moved in 1815, leaving his daughter Sarah and her husband Thomas Waring (married 1803), in residence at Hewitts. Meanwhile the Petleys were sinking. In 1783 Charles's estate was divided between his two sons, John and Ralph. Ralph got Hewitts. He had married in 1778 another Elizabeth, a Scottish woman, daughter of Dr. Alexander Campbell. Ralph died after only ten years but had three sons. The eldest son Charles got an estate based on the family home at Riverhead while the younger brothers Horace and John Cade inherited Hewitts subject to their mother's interest for life.

John Cade, born in 1783 became a Lieutenant Colonel in the Royal Artillery. When stationed in Spain he met and married Louisa Valverde de Calderon. Horace joined the Navy and became a Lieutenant. He became very financially embarrassed and was bailed out by his mother on more than one occasion. If that wasn't enough his brother ran up debts with various tradesmen. Elizabeth was a generous woman and perhaps too generous when it came to her sons; so when she died in 1825 economies had to be made.

John Fuller died in 1819 leaving two daughters. When Hewitts came up for sale towards the end of 1826 it was purchased by trustees for the benefit of daughter Sarah, for £2,788 (the estate eventually went to her husband Thomas Waring). Their great-grandson William Arthur Waring moved back to "Hewitts" after the sale of "Woodlands" in 1922. He died in 1945 and the Hewitts estate was disposed of by the family. A large part of it ended up with Cadbury Schweppes.

In front of the old farmhouse is a barn on mushroom shaped stilts designed to keep rats from gaining access from the underside. There is a large dilapidated barn opposite at Bluebell Farm. A period looking sign at the entrance indicates the premises of M. Hogben & Sons. Walking up the road you come to Hewitts Farm Cottages, formerly Bo-Peep Cottages. There is a modern pair followed by another 1860's pair built for William Waring's employees. Note they all had good size gardens where his tenants could grow produce for their own consumption. Both have large modern extensions.

Outside the Bo-Peep pub there is a R3 bus stop if you wish to end your walk here. The pub serves good food and is open all day.

Chelsfield Downs

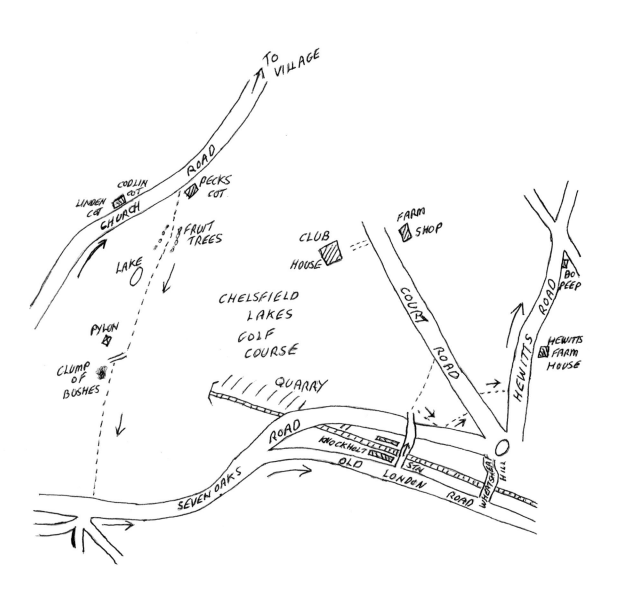

Poor quality but rare photograph of Halstead (Knockholt) with original buildings and a full staff!
(Philip Lane collection)

1960's view of Knockholt. Note the "Wheatsheaf" signal box.
(Philip Lane collection)

Saturday 16th April 2011 at Knockholt. The 11.18 Sevenoaks train approaches. No one waits but some may want to get off. Let's hope they take all their personal possessions with them and not leave any parcels unattended on the station as it may be a while before anyone finds them.

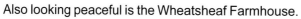

Also looking peaceful is the Wheatsheaf Farmhouse.

Mr Bowen's timber being loaded (or unloaded) at the station yard.
(Philip Lane collection)

Aerial view of Chelsfield in 1975. It can clearly be seen how the A224 bisects the village.

The White Hart. Renamed the Bo-Peep in 1971.

A recent picture showing not a great deal of change.

Well Hill

A walk of about 3½ miles with ½ mile to transport at the end

The Bo-Peep displays 1500 as the date of establishment but this is highly debatable. The oldest part, whatever age that is, has a number of seemingly uncoordinated extensions. The official name until 1971 was The White Hart but for many years it had been known locally as the Bo-Peep after the area which means view point or look-out point. Once grocery was also sold here. Inside there is a nice big old fireplace.

We are on a corner of the Maypole Triangle to which we will return. Before venturing to Well Hill on foot it is well to note there are no public transport links and no remaining pubs, so you will be on your own. Make sure you have good walking shoes or boots, have appropriate clothing for the likely weather and carry at least a bottle of water. You should not get lost with my directions but you may wish to take an Ordnance Survey map.

Turn right into Shoreham Lane to pass another pair of Hewitts cottages which first appeared on the electoral register in 1955 but look a few years earlier. Then go left over a stile, (the footpath opposite to the right runs parallel to Hewitts Road though an equestrian area and then right to the roundabout with the A21/A224). Cross the field and then the stile in the opposite left corner. The path continues beside the hedge to another stile then bears right to a third. On the way you get a view of Kilnfields on the left. The first three blocks of four, to the right, were built after World War 1 as "Homes for heroes" but described officially as "Houses for the Working Classes". The land, of 1 acre 28 perches, was purchased from A. T. Waring in 1919/20 for the sum of around £100. The Borough architect F. Danby Smith drew up the plans. While the local authority acted with commendable speed in locating and buying land, here and at other locations in the district, and getting plans drawn up, the project was delayed by the haggling over costs by the London Housing Board and an entanglement of red tape more obstructive than the barbed wire on the Western front. A "hero" wanting a house here had to wait a few years. To mid 1927 in fact when C. A. George & Co. erected them for a cost of £350 each without fences paths etc. At a B. R. D. C. meeting on 22nd November they were described as "eminently satisfactory".

In the allocation of tenancies, preferences were given to working parishioners and the initial rent set at 7s per week. The first tenant of number 5 requested permission to retain two rabbits which had been pets for long periods. Permission was granted subject to the animals being kept in a cleanly condition so as not to cause a nuisance. Unfortunately for the poor rabbits this condition was not adhered to and permission was later revoked. The tenant allocated number 7 proved "undesirable" and his tenancy immediately cancelled.

Cross the third stile and take the path that leads to Rock Hill. The early 19th cent Rock and Fountain, of two storeys and basement, red brick with grey headers has a single story weatherboard extension. Neighbouring "Rock Cottage" was once a pair of two story weatherboard homes with matching lean to extension. The former pub is converted to residential accommodation and a new house is to be built in the former car park. At the entrance to this car park is a large vertical rock, which, when the establishment was open, had water piped to run down and this was illuminated at night. Whether this will be put back into service remains to be seen.

In front of the former pub is one of Sir Giles Gilbert Scott's K6 red phone boxes of 1935, one of half a dozen or so in the Chelsfield area, in roads and gardens. The shape is said to be based on that of the tomb of Sir John Soane in old St. Pancras Cemetery.

Walk up Rock Hill; the houses and bungalows here date from the 1920's to recent times. You pass the entrance to High Beech Farm and turn into Well Hill Lane. Most homes are relatively modern with a few older and there are some of interest like Ashdown a weatherboard bungalow. Chelsfield Covered Reservoir and Booster Station is the approximate site of a windmill marked on a map of 1777 but this was probably an embellishment. Goat Hill Farm looks impressive. It is basically two stories and attic, facing west, said to be of "period" origins; (period is a word used by estate agents to describe anything conceived before 1970), although I'm told it was once extremely dilapidated and there can't be much "period" left. It has been considerably modernised and extended but all the same the work has been tastefully done and looks the part from a distance. With various outbuildings the farm extends to about 15 acres. By complete contrast next door is a tiny single story cottage called Appledore.

Attractive Bramble Cottage is followed by Hollow Dene (c.1996) which has a wildlife lake and woodland in its private garden but nature lovers can take the nearby entrance into Pascall's Wood, a Woodland Trust area for a circular walk.

Additional Walk 1
About 1½ miles

Some of the route is bridle path which can become muddy in winter but not enough to worry the seasoned walker.

For this suggested walk, take the left hand track and at the next junction turn right. The path straight on goes past a radio mast and over the M25 approach, to Hollows Wood and Chelsfield Lane, Badgers Mount. It is worth walking a short distance this way for the views each side where the telephone lines cross the path. In the direction of our walk the track follows power lines for a distance before turning away. Go straight on at the next junction and you come out on Chelsfield Lane which will become Shoreham Lane as you walk up. To the left it goes under the M25 approach; we turn right and pass another entrance to the Wood with a farm yard of indeterminate use opposite, surrounded by the trees of Conyearth Wood; (cony means rabbit). Take the next entrance to the right back into Pascall's Wood. Just before this is a view to the left over an equestrian centre towards Hewitts. Left at the crossways of paths and you come back to Well Hill Lane.

Returning to the top of Well Hill Lane there is a footpath between the top two bungalows on the east side. Just over the stile you can get a good view over the Darent valley. The path goes right and then left, but can become overgrown and impassable. If that is the case go straight down the hill from the top stile towards the gates and stile at the opposite side. The ground is uneven, so take care. If you don't feel up to it just go to the top of Well Hill Lane and turn right.

The path comes out on a track leading to Westwood Farm. The path opposite heads off towards the M25 and is of no interest. Left on the track brings you to the bottom of Rock Hill opposite Firmingers Road, probably named after a family of that name. On the corners are the entrances to Fountain Farm and Nursery and Woodyholme Nursery, specializing in seasonal bedding plants. Unless you are interested in buying plants there is not much to detain you here, so walk up Rock Hill to the homes towards the top. They include "Tanglewood", a square modernist house, "Valley View" and "Duna", two weatherboard bungalows, "Homelands" (1996), a modern bungalow with landscaped grounds, and "Robins", an imposing house of the 1930's. There was once a strawberry farm here.

Opposite Well Hill Lane is Well Hill (the road). Up to the "Y" junction where the road divides from the other direction, the dwelling are all fairly recent. At the junction is a Shoreham Parish Council notice board. Part of Well Hill was once in Old Chelsfield but it is now all in the Shoreham Parish of Sevenoaks District Council, which does it no good. The boundary of Chelsfield Ecclesiastical Parish was extended east in 1938 to include the whole of Well Hill to what is now the approximate position of the M25 and remains the same today. Confused? Never mind just enjoy your surroundings.

"Prospect Cottage" sits neatly opposite the junction. To the left all the properties are newish. Alwin's, the general store once stood on this stretch of road but is now gone. Turn right for the old part of Well Hill. After more recent bungalows and the entrance to Kingshall Farm you come to "Well Hill House". Built in 1895 it has an impressive entrance porch and its viewing gallery above the roof is the highest point in Well Hill. It is said that Westminster and St. Paul's can be seen from here. Its large grounds have an annexe, tennis courts and swimming pool.

A short distance further on a drive to the right leads to Well Hill Mission Church, built in 1893 and dedicated on June 22nd that year, on land presented by Sir William Hart Dyke of Lullingstone. It was designed by Spencer Chadwick who did a good job considering the limited budget available. It is said to have been intended for hop pickers but locals must have appreciated it too, as it is quite a long walk either to St. Martin's or Shoreham and back. It was built for Shoreham Parish but is now in the Chelsfield Parish. There are services on some Sundays and it is open for occasional special events. If you wish to see inside please check for dates displayed or in the Parish Magazine (see St Martin's section).

The interior is well worth seeing as it is of a rustic and homely appearance with much use made of timber as you would expect. The small pews came from another church that was being decommissioned but fit in here as if made for it. Among the small collection of plaques is a smart brass one for Robert Ashington Pullen, Vicar of Shoreham 1888-1896 and in office when the church was built. There is a Roll of Honour for 1939-1945. New cushions and kneelers have recently been made. Work on the kneelers, by local church members, began in the centenary year 1993 and the designs show local landmarks and the seasons within the outlines of church windows from Well Hill, Chelsfield and Shoreham churches.

The estate of Lullingstone once extended to some 10,000 acres and included the Manor of Great Orpington and land in Farnbourgh and stretched to Knockholt in the southerly direction. Lullingstone has been in the possession of the Hart or Hart Dyke family since the 16th century when the dissolution of the monasteries provided most of the land. Bad fortune and death duties has shrunk the estate dramatically, particularly during the 20th century, and it is now under 100 acres although the Hart Dykes still remain in their Castle.

Continue along the path past "Viewlands" to Firmingers Road. The path opposite goes to Park Gate near the M25. A short distance to the right is "Firmingers Wells", a brick and flint house extended in complementary style. Turn back uphill past Dean's Piggery and Daisy Farm. "Rosedene" is a house of recent times but with tiled frontage in arts and crafts style, followed by "Oak Cottage" in old style weatherboard.

You come back to Well Hill and turn right for Green Hills Farm, the house is 19th cent, partly rebuilt, and you get good views from this road over the motorway towards Lullingstone Park. At the corner of Parkgate Road is "Chestnut Cottage", tile-hung with wisteria covered walls and looks great when the plant is in flower. The road descends past Springbank Farm and over the motorway to an interesting group of buildings. 19th cent "Parkgate Cottages", a rag-stone barn conversion, "Pond Cottage" and "Parkgate House", formerly Parkgate Farmhouse. Built by the Hart Dykes in the first part of the 18th century, it was one of seven, the others being East Hall near St Mary Cray, Home Farm, Eynsford, Cockerhurst, Shoreham, Wested, Crockenhill, and Petham Court and Pedham, both Swanley. This one is two storeys and attic in red brick with later tile hung extension. The road continues to Lullingstone Park Golf Course.

Cross back over the motorway; the footpath on the south is the one from Firmingers Road and the one on the north leads to Crockenhill. At the top of Parkgate Road go straight on and downhill to Daltons Road. Opposite on the left "The Homstead" is fairly recent, mock Tudor with tile panels. Daltons Road name-board has Chelsfield in small letters underneath to remind us that after all this walking we are still there. Up here is Skeet Hill Farm. This farm and other land in the area was bought by Kent County Council c1922 for the purpose of creating smallholdings and new cottages were built at various locations.

The farmhouse, behind the "Old Barn" is probably 20th cent. but Skeet Hill Farm Cottages are 19th cent. and are neighboured by "Willow Cottage", appearing compact from the front with some timbering but considerably extended to the rear. It looks quite a pleasing group. There are a pair of cottages called "Corncroft" about a quarter mile on but these are late 20th cent. and of no real interest apart from a view across the fields opposite. The road continues to Crockenhill. Return towards Skeet Hill and take a short footpath to the right which cuts off the corner. Opposite is "Skeet Hill Cottage", late 19th cent. brick with slate roof. Skeet Hill was originally called Skid Hill. Skid meant "pasture where slips of wood, or billets, are collected".

To the right is "Skeet Hill House" of Dutch gabled appearance, about 100 years old. Now it is an activity centre for Jewish children, it was purchased by The Brady Boys Club in 1943 as a respite from the dangers of the East End of London. It is set in seven acres with sports amenities including an obstacle course built by the Army Corps of Engineers and a campsite. The house has been modernised and can sleep about 70. Open not only to Jewish children but also other faiths including Moslems.

You can return to a footpath on the right past the gate to "Beech Tree Cottage" and go left through the kissing gate, or do the additional walk to Crown Wood.

Additional Walk 2
About 1½ miles

Continue along Skeet Hill Lane and into Gorse Road on the right. On the right of Skeet Hill Lane a sign welcomes you to the London Borough of Bromley while a sign on the left warns you that you would be entering a Low Emission Zone and you should make sure your exhaust complies with regulations, but as we are not going this way it doesn't matter. In Gorse Road you enter into Crown Wood. Crownwood Farmhouse appears to be 20th cent. The footpath crossing here is the Chelsfield Circular which is a walk from Chelsfield but having a good part outside of this area. To the north-east it runs beside Crown Wood towards Crockenhill, but you go south-west over the stile towards Chelsfield. You pass through a field which usually has horses in and right of a fence to a kissing gate. At Skeet Hill Lane turn left. The house at Micklewood Farm looks early 20th cent.

Walk along the Lane until you see a footpath marked on the right up some steps. A little further on the Lane you will see "Woodside Farm" house, white painted probably 19th cent and next door Whiteheads plant nursery. From the steps the path goes right then left across a field to a hedgerow and turns right again. At the end of the hedgerow turn sharp left across another field. You will see a marker about half way. You come to Doctor's Wood. Don't let the Private Wood sign put you off, there is a footpath marker here; enter the wood and take the branch to the left. When you come out turn right, go around the edge of the field to the left and you come to a gap in the hedge and some steps up to the path. Here you can see the recently rebuilt "Beech Tree Cottage". Continue down the path and through two kissing gates to link up with the main walk.

The path goes uphill left of a pylon. It sounds as if you could fry your lunch on it but please don't try. Cross a stile and the path passes to the other side of Green Hills Farm. Two more stiles and you arrive at a very nice terrace of cottages, once known as the Black Cottages c.1858, and said to have been built for the farm now called Green Hills.

A path next to the right-hand end of the terrace takes you through to an open space which was once the Well Hill hamlet's centre (some here refer to it as a village). On your extreme right stood until recently the Kent Hounds pub. Sadly demolished in 2010 to make way for a new modernist house which will probably not stand here for half the time span of its predecessor. The pub was originally a beer house, first mentioned in 1867, and as the Kent Hounds in 1870 which closed in 2006. There was a pub sign on the green with benches and seats for customers; there was a general store nearby and a bakery just across the road. All that remains of the once heart of the community is a patch of grass and some fir trees which partially conceal the only public amenity left, a row of recycling bins. After seeing the remains of the Kent Hounds site I thought of the following verse:-

> All things must pass,
> We know it's true.
> They breathe their last,
> And fade from view.
> The mists of time,
> Which twist and curl,
> Take the memories that swirl.
> Brick and stone,
> And blood and bone,
> And all that came from sweat and toil,
> Once again returns to soil.

Pump Lane, formerly Back Hill was once the main street of the old community and part of the old boundary between Chelsfield and Shoreham. The Bromley part of Well Hill was transferred to Sevenoaks Council who don't seem to be bothered with it, content to let it become a residential out-post of its administration. This is the inevitable result of centralization in local politics. Pump Lane should have been made a conservation area, there are less deserving holders of this title.

Walk over to Well Hill; to the left opposite is the perhaps late 18th cent. weatherboard "Oaktree Cottage". A bakery, one of two in the hamlet, was located to its rear which was towards the road where a small brick building can be seen. Brick and flint Stonehouse Farmhouse is opposite "Claremont", a single story weatherboard house. In the other direction on the corner of Pump Lane is a probably early 20th cent house, half hidden by foliage. On the other side are "Springcroft", New Forge, where decorative ironwork is produced and "Hilltop" which looks 1920's.

Go back to Pump Lane and start down to pass modern "Bower House" and probably late 18th or early 19th cent "Hollyden". After another couple of modern properties, a bungalow and "The Poplars", (c1996) a mixture of mock Tudor and tile-hung, you pass a drive to Owen's Farm, situated in Owen's Wood. A footpath on the left would take you back to Well Hill

Continue down the hill and much modernised and extended "Maryleigh Cottage", thought to have been built in 1848 as two farm workers cottages, converted to one home in 1967 and extended to the rear. The remaining old houses in the Lane are 18th cent; "Well Hill Cottage" and "Spring Cottage", both brick and flint with tile-hung upper stories. They have ornamental wells in their gardens but the original was where "Well Hill Cottage's" garden is situated. This is, of course, the well from which the area got its name. The ornamental replacement appears to be slightly higher than the original. Although the working well is gone water still runs from the bank, I'm told, even in the driest weather.

The residents used to rely on this water source, not too bad if you lived at the bottom of the hill but quite a trek if you had to struggle to the top with a couple of bucketfuls. This water supply was used well, (pun intended), into the 20th century.

From B.R.D.C. minutes of March 8th 1910:—

"Read letter dated 2nd instant...........enclosing copy of Analysts Report upon a sample of drinking water taken from the public well at Well Hill, Chelsfield and that as it appeared desirable that such wells should be protected from surface pollution he has obtained two tenders for the execution of the necessary work. It was resolved that of Mr. James Smith of Chelsfield.........for the sum of £9. 15s. 0d be accepted." Mr. Smith did further work here in 1914 but this time only charged £4 15s. Mains water finally came to Well Hill or part of it in 1923.

At the bottom of Pump Hill we have returned to the Rock and Fountain. What a pity it's not still open. A drive on the right is the main entrance to Owen's Farm which specializes in pine furniture. If you wish to end your walk here the nearest bus stop is at the other end of Hawstead Lane.

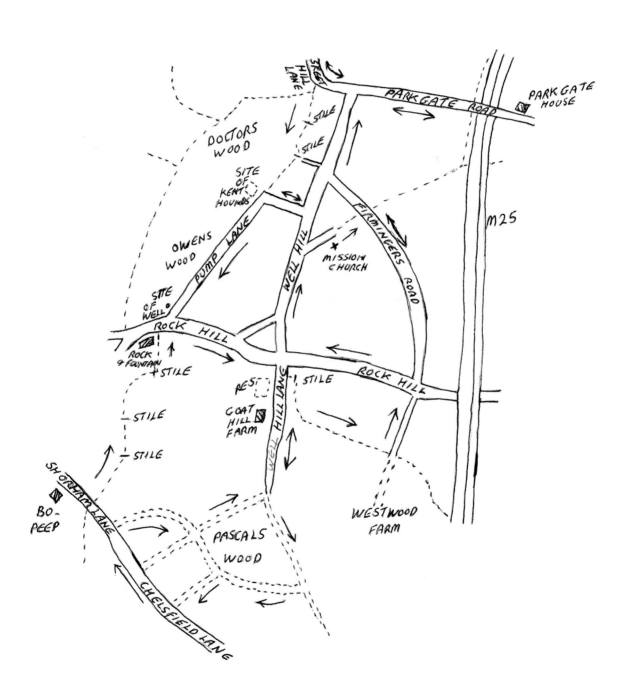

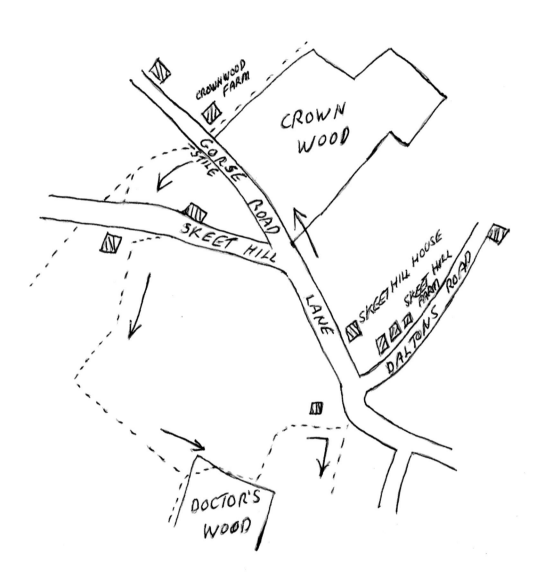

The viewing gallery of "Well Hill House". London landmarks can be seen from there.

Well Hill Mission Church, an excellently proportioned small building.

The homely interior of Well Hill Church.

The "Black Cottages", no longer black which must be an improvement.

The Kent Hounds pub at Well Hill.
(Philip Lane collection)

Autumn 2010. The Kent Hounds is nearly gone.

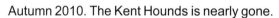

Alwin's was the general store, also gone.
(Philip Lane collection)

The rear of "Oaktree Cottage" which faces away from the road. A bakery once traded here.

The Rock and Fountain, judging from the age of the car, in the 1920's.
(Philip Lane collection)

A recent picture of the Rock and Fountain, now serving as residential accommodation.

Pump Lane (or Back Hill) probably around 1900.
(Philip Lane collection)

Collecting water from the pump was a daily task.
(Geoffrey Copus collection)

Water flowing from the bank below the site of the pump in Pump Lane.

Water not flowing down the rock near the former pub car park entrance. Will it run again?

Around the Maypole

A walk of about 1¼ miles

To maintain continuity I will start where the last section of the walk left off at the bottom of Pump Hill, but you can also start this stage at the village end of Hawstead Lane where there is a R3 bus stop and walk towards Well Hill doing the last described section first.

The red brick and weatherboard house at the junction of Jubilee Road is called "Four Ways", as three roads and a footpath converge here. The path goes up to Doctor's Wood and joins the paths we used at Well Hill. Owen's Farm can be seen on the hillside.

Turn into Jubilee Road. Just into the road is a pair of extended cottages called "The Firs". One is brick and weatherboard and the other is now mock Tudor! They were built for William Waring as labourers cottages in the late 1860's. Longlands Farm follows, the residence being a modern bungalow.

A group of cottages faces you on the corner of Hollybush Lane, two pairs, "Maypole Cottages" fronting Jubilee Road and a detached, "Yew Tree Cottage", in Hollybush Lane which we turn into. They were built for Sophia Harris who inherited the land and replaced some run-down property with these, new in 1897. Chelsfield seems to have been well stocked with landlords who provided good homes for their workers and Percival Bowen was one. "Hollybush Cottages", originally "Black Cottages", because they were painted black were one of his developments. Built in 1898 and of good size for their day. Mr. Bowen being a timber merchant it is not surprising that they are of timber construction. Now painted white which must I think be an improvement. You now see the frontage of "Kilnfields", the later ones further up are red brick, some tile-hung, built c1950's.

Walk past the front of "Hollybush Cottages" and go through to Maypole Road. Just before this on your right was the site of the poor houses, in more ways than one. Each Parish was required to support its own needy and although Chelsfield never had very many some were accommodated, if that's the word, here. Local charities and the Church would help out when they could. The site now forms part of a garden.

On your left is "Hollycroft", designed by George St Pierre Harris and built in 1912 for William Fox and his sister Catherine after their retirement from running Lilly's Farm. "Willy" was related to the Fox family brewers of Green Street Green. Nowadays there is boarding for cats here. Chelsfield is a nice place for a holiday if you are a cat or even if you're not, but you'd have trouble finding a hotel room.

"Osbornes", the small farmhouse opposite has the date 1705, when it was rebuilt to replace an earlier house. When Peter Collett, a merchant tailor of London and the first known owner of Lillys Farm, died in 1607 his widow gave "Osborns" to the Church to provide income to maintain the magnificent St John's Chapel, the Collett monument there, and for charity. The Eleemosynary Charity of Joanna Collett still provides funds today.

On the corner as you enter Jubilee Road is 19th cent "Maypole Cottage", followed by "Rochberie", a modern bungalow with attractive bay windows.

"Yew Tree House" was built in the 1950's replacing an ancient timber-framed house. The story goes that the owner being unable to afford the cost of renovation and modernisation reluctantly demolished it, despite being 500 hundred years old and listed; (what is the point of listing anything if you can still pull it down?). It was said to have been built from ships timbers obtained from Deptford and although it had no apparent foundations was as solid as a rock until the day it was forcibly removed. Writer Derek Sheffield's grandparents once lived here and he managed to squeeze three books out of their life and adventures. Their down to earth stories can be read in "This Forgotten Place", (surely not), "And Then There Were None" and "Until The End of Time".

After another modern bungalow and a pair of red brick cottages built by Mary Fuller in 1824, you will come back to "Maypole Cottages". Return to Maypole Road and turn right. To the right of the road is Maypole railed pond in which you might find water during the winter months but often contains mud or is dry. An R3 bus stop is nearby. A bit further along is a terrace of mid-Victorian cottages called Chalk Row, which originally adjoined a chalk hole or chalk pit here. On the end is a former pub, originally the Maple beer house, at one time also known as Smith's Ale House. It later became the Maypole Arms. There is still an iron sign fixed to the wall which may have been a pub sign and now bears the name "Maple House".

Just beyond the terrace a footpath gives access to fields once known as Eighteen Acres. You can reach three destinations from here, the village recreation ground, the Church or Hewitts shop. Keeping to the road you reach "Mount Hall" which is late 18th cent brick and part tile-hung and opposite is Bucks Cross farmhouse, rebuilt c1850, at the rear of its wonderfully ramshackle looking farmyard which you pass as you turn the corner to the right into Hawstead Lane. There is no such place as Hawstead but a possible origin for the name may come from "hawe", a hedged enclosure, and so be "place of hedged enclosure". Hedged enclosures were used to trap animals which when driven in through the only entrance and could not then escape.

Bucks Cross Farm belonged to the Petley family until it passed out of their hands around 1668. A footpath on the left leads north and then turns east to the woods at Well Hill. Once known as Durleys Lane and used for driving livestock to and from the adjacent fields.

Preceding Brown's School is the modern headmaster's (or headmistress's) house. The school is based on the former Waring family home "Woodlands" now called "Cannock House" It was built for John Fuller in 1815 and he lived here until his death in 1819. His daughter Mary stayed on here until her death in 1842. Far from taking a back seat, she took a strong interest in the running of the estate. Thomas Waring, her brother-in-law purchased the Manor of Chelsfield and the Court Lodge estate in 1844. "Woodlands" subsequently became the family residence.

Thomas Waring was a descendant of Richard Waring and Catherine, daughter of Rev. William Wall, Vicar of Shoreham for 53 years from 1674. They had eighteen children most of whom lived into adulthood. Tragically Thomas Waring and his wife Sarah were not so lucky and of eleven children only one, William, survived his father who died in 1851. Family sources blamed typhoid from a defective water supply for their misfortune. William must either have had luck or a stronger constitution as he lived to the age of 86.

William Waring

Born in 1818, he was educated at Rowes Academy in Bromley, a rather strict boarding school, which he may not have liked too much but must gone some way in preparing him for estate management. After inheriting he became what could be a role-model for the benevolent country squire in any T.V. costume drama. He became involved in many aspects of local life and a member of the West Kent Hunt and the Agricultural Association. He was J.P. at Locks Bottom Petty Sessions and was on the bench with Charles Darwin, a distant cousin, on occasions between 1859 and 1862.

He took a genuine interest in the welfare of his employees and improving the lot of farm labourers was his favourite subject for speeches at Association events. A job with Mr. Waring may not have been the best in the world but was a good deal better than many and provided you didn't expect luxuries like Bank Holidays off, (they weren't for you), so long as you knew your place and you kept your nose clean (metaphorically not actually), it was well worth a little extra effort to keep it. You would have the opportunity of renting a good cottage, of a good size for the day with a garden and if anything happened to you your family would not be thrown out in the lane. Perhaps fair treatment of his workers was the key to Mr. Waring's successful business methods.

William was married in 1843 to Mary Wall Tasker daughter of brewer John Tasker. They had five sons and six daughters. Two of the children died young but this generation fared better than the last.

William often paid visits to the village school, where his daughters taught on a voluntary basis, and he sometimes found it necessary to lecture pupils concerning incidents of "inappropriate" behaviour.

He was succeeded by his son Arthur Thomas when he died in 1904. Daughter Anne married Rector Folliott Baugh, who while about thirty-six years older still out-lived her.

More information on the Waring family and other Chelsfield matters are given in "Chelsfield Chronicles" by the eminent local historian Mr. Geoffrey Copus.

William's son Arthur Thomas was also a J.P. and served on the County and local Councils being very active in committee work, as indeed was his son William Arthur, (like many other families of the time they had a passion for re-cycling names), who down-sized to Hewitts in 1922, auctioning a large part of the contents of "Woodlands". The house, which at this time still had no mains gas or electricity, was sold to a Mr Tomkins, there to the 1940's and later coming into the possession of Morleys, manufacturers of gloves, who used it for staff accommodation. Cannock School, an independent boys grammar school was established here in 1960. Brown's is now a private school catering for special needs pupils.

If the front gates are open you can see the mansion beyond. Stables, cottages and other 19th century out buildings are to the front and right side. The school later diversified into nursery education as can be seen when we move on and pass the recent outbuildings for this use.

After "The Bungalow", built by Mr Tomkins, a plain (probably 1930) home you come upon a marvellous sight, a whole collection of traditional farm buildings; a farmhouse, a dower house, oast houses, stables, barns, the lot, all lovingly maintained and looking just like new. Well...... actually...... that's because they are new, at least c2002, built by Asprey Homes of Sevenoaks and designed by architect Nigel J. Bradbury. and called Home Farm.

The site, originally parts of Plantation and Well fields which were part of Bucks Cross Farm and more recently Woodlands Farm, had been a car breakers for about thirty years and extensive soil testing was required before any residential building could take place. Breakers like the one here were once common. All that was needed was a spare field and you were in business, buying up old cars for next to nothing, reselling a few that could be repaired, and dismantling the rest providing a source of cheap spares for inexpensive motoring. Then one day along comes the dreaded "health and safety" officer who informs you of regulations which mean you would need a hard standing and have to dispose of various substances and materials by the correct methods. By the time you had complied with these and all the other unforeseen requirements there would be no profit left and so you might as well shut up shop and sell the land for development. Many of these yards closed this way.

Perhaps after about 50 years these new buildings will have weathered into their surroundings.

In "This Forgotten Place" Derek Sheffield records that during World War 11 a Hurricane pilot made a forced landing in the next field. He climbed from the plane unhurt, telephoned his base and was back in the air the same day.

If you have completed this section of the walk return to Maypole Road; if you started there continue to Jubilee Road.

Maypole and Village

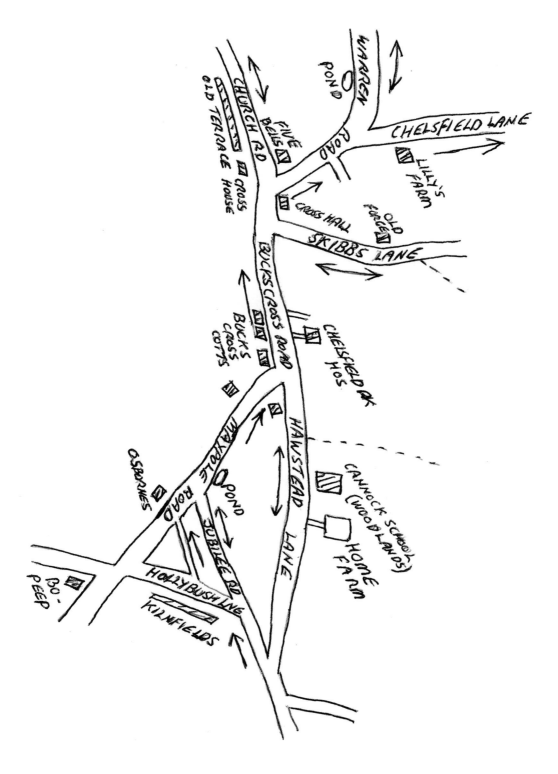

A picturesque "Fourways" in Hawstead Lane.

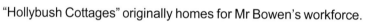

"Hollybush Cottages" originally homes for Mr Bowen's workforce.

Home Farm looks pretty but is almost new. The farmhouse even has fake blocked windows.

Kilnfields have been personalized since construction.

"Osbornes". The farm still earns money for good causes today although there aren't many poor to help in Chelsfield today as most residents live quite comfortably.

The former Maypole Arms at the end of Chalk Row Terrace.

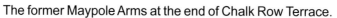

William Waring looking every bit the typical
country squire. (Geoffrey Copus collection)

"Woodlands", now known as "Cannock House", the courtyard crowded with outbuildings.

The Village

A walk of about 1 mile

Where the village starts and ends is a matter of opinion but for convenience I am starting at the corner of Maypole Road in the area known as Bucks Cross. In Bucks Cross Road just before the R3 bus stop, standing out not so much like a sore thumb but more like a computer generated image superimposed on an old photograph, is another intrusive low emission zone sign. It must have been put here for a good reason but it would be better somewhere else.

Directly opposite is one of the most ancient houses in Chelsfield. It is listed 16th cent but is almost certainly earlier, of timber-framed construction and weatherboard with some brick or tile-work probably later to the lower ground floor. From the road it appears to have sunk slightly into the ground. It was probably the home of a lady called Alice Bray who died in 1509 after meticulously planning her funeral in her will and as she was the sister of the previous Rector, Richard Bonaventure, it was no doubt meticulously carried out. Her gifts to the Church included a small field, "Bell Ropes Field", the income from which was to provide income for the purchase of bell ropes. Although the field was sold in 1886 the invested money still pays for bell ropes today.

Next come a couple of cottages, not a pair as 4 is bigger than 3, and these are brick and flint 18th cent. Opposite is the original entrance to "Chelsfield House", two sections of ruined wall looking quite picturesque. A tree lined drive led to the house from here. The next two cottages are a pair, c1740, brick, tile-hung with weatherboard elevations. I think the attic rooms are later additions as they were workers cottages and unlikely to have had three storeys originally.

Chelsfield House

"Chelsfield House" also known as the "Old Rectory" is now the main part of Chelsfield Park Hospital, (it is of course not in Chelsfield Park as we know this to be elsewhere). There has been a Rectory or Parson's house on the site from at least 1442, but the one existing in the early 19th century was not good enough for the Rev. Doctor John Edward Tarleton D.C.L., so he had a new one built between 1834/38 probably using money which came to him from his wealthy family. The family seat was Bolesworth Castle in Cheshire. The Rev. Doctor was educated at Eton and Oxford, became a Fellow of All Souls in 1809 and they presented him with the "living" in 1834. His home was said to be stuffed with good furniture and paintings and "pleasure" gardens surrounded it. One wonders what the occupant of "Woodlands" must have thought of her ostentatious neighbour. Rich clergymen were not unusual at that time but are few and far between today. Despite, or maybe because of his moneyed upbringing the good Doctor did not have much idea of financial management and towards the end of his Rector-ship his outgoings seem to have over taken his means. When he died in office in 1849, intestate, he was found to have substantial debts; his affairs taking years to sort out.

The Rectory was sold by the Church and was later bought by Edward Norman, a partner in Martin's Bank. The Normans' family home was "The Rookery" at Bromley Common although they had extensive holdings including Elmstead Woods which was used for shooting. The family gave their name to Norman Park in Bromley. Edward was the ninth child of George Ward and Sibella Norman. Edward, who died in 1923 made numerous additions and refinements to the house and had new stables and lodges built. Additional land was acquired around the home, the estate growing to about 60 acres and the family, later the Norman-Butlers, stayed here until 1939.

"Chelsfield House" was requisitioned by the Army during 1939-1945 as a centre for the rehabilitation of wounded soldiers and barracks for those manning gun emplacements. After the war it was used as a halfway house for people who had lost their homes due to bombing, the building being converted to flats, 11 shown occupied on the 1958 voters' register. It became derelict for a while before someone tried turning it into a luxury hotel but the venture failed. In fact it seemed doomed from the start for soon after the plans had been approved a fire gutted the east wing on 17th March 1972. The Chelsfield Park Hotel and Le Gourmet Restaurant did not last long and now the hospital is here.

Approaching from the road towards reception the old house in solid red brick is to the right with newer extensions, complementary but not matching, to the left. Walls and steps of the landscaped gardens still exist to the front.

After the Hospital grounds a short unnamed track leads past the 19th cent. "The Lodge" to The Gardens, former out buildings of "Chelsfield House" all in red brick. It is also possible to cut through from the Hospital gardens. They were all built for Edward Norman. Number 2 was coach house and stables with the adjacent ground used as a kitchen garden for the estate. Like the main house the outbuildings were used for bomb victims after W. W. 2 and then in the 1960's the they were taken over by Kent County Council and rented out, 2 being used as a nursery for a time and eventually they were sold into private hands.

As you approach the village centre the railings guarding the ditch to the right are similar to those lining the bypass and probably date from the same late 20's period. A child's play area is fronted by the Village sign. Designed by George Rose the Village Hall is opposite, c1953, weatherboard with small central clock-tower carrying a weather-vane. Beside this is the Recreation Ground with a timber pavilion. This pavilion stands on the site of an air-raid post and there is still a shelter underneath. An excellent Fair is held here every year which includes a flying display organised by the Chelsfield Flying Club, (I am still trying to locate Chelsfield airport).

Right into Skibbs Lane and on the left are the Parish Room and the current Rectory (1962) which Dr Tarleton may have found use for as a summer house. Next, on the right is another lodge of "Chelsfield House", recently threatened with demolition, it is now being restored and extended. After a while you come to "Hurstdene", c1900, built by village blacksmith Hubert Blackwell who leased the land in 1897. It has a fan-lighted front door and Tudor beaming to the upper floor, an unusual combination His works premises still remain to the rear now used by Lockyer Motors, test and repair centre. The original blacksmith's shop is brick with a galvanised paint shop over topped with a slate roof. Carts were made on the ground floor and hoisted above for painting. Across the yard is the shed where horses were shoed and, close to wall, set into the surface of the yard is the circular stone on which wheels were made.

If following the main walk return to Bucks Cross Road.

Additional Walk 3
About 2 miles.

Continue up Skibbs Lane to footpath FP 211 (Chelsfield Circular) on the right. Cross the field to Black Bush Wood. It might have been much bigger once but is now an odd shape, so you go through one part, left along the edge, take the path to the right and across a field to another part of the wood and through this to emerge in another field. Right and immediately left will take you to Skeet Hill Lane on the west side of Micklewood Farm, getting a good view of Cookham Farm to the left and Well Hill to the right.

Turn left at the end of the path onto the Lane and the first house you come to is "Heatheroof", a farmhouse, probably early 20th cent and like the majority of homes on this stretch has a rough rendered finish. The road can get flooded just past here so you may have to take to the bank. Continuing on you come to "Cookham Farm" house on the left and "Woodlands" (another one) opposite. Cookham, first mentioned in 1241 as Cokham; means "Cook settlement " - settlement maybe after a person called Cok. The next cottage whose name I could not find is probably late 19th cent. Another 19th cent cottage can be seen across a field to the right. Go past Cookham Hill Farm and house to the junction with Skibbs Lane.

Right here and you come to a "Hazeldene of Chelsfield" notice. The whole site is surrounded by a high fence and all that can be glimpsed is a modern building with tile-hanging and fussy roofing. It is set in an area called Sage Wents. I think "Wents" means "ways". Opposite is the cottage that could be seen from Skeet Hill Lane but very difficult to view here. It is followed opposite by modern house "Oaklands" and a 19th cent cottage. Further along past the entrance to Tanglewood Farm there more late 19th or early 20th cottages, detached at "Brambles", Byways Nursery and Watts Farm and a pair also at Watts Farm, all being white rendered.

Turn back towards the Village and over the crossroads (into the low emission zone again). Along the way you can view, through the hedge on the right, Goddington; the Park and "Goddington House" can be seen. You pass a coal post inscribed 24 & 25 VIC CAP 42; (for more on coal posts see Goddington section). An unmarked footpath opposite leads to Lillys Wood. Continue on the Lane back to the Village.

A redundant bus shelter has a smaller copy of the War Memorial plaque we will see later at the church. Attractive 18th cent red brick Cross House, and Wyche House are next. The Village Post Office was here until it went the same way as many others; (my opinion about that can be guessed). To the left of these buildings in an old outbuilding with a wonderfully warped roof which looks as if it is about to fall in but is probably as solid as a rock. In front of Cross House is a red phone box placed here in the Post Office days.

On the same side of the Church Road, the Village's main street, is a mainly white-painted terrace, the first part dating from the 1600's. The first and longest unit carrying the name "Neals". It was Thompson's before Neal's and this was for many years the Village store, you can see where the shop windows were but the entrance door has gone. In its very early days it was an inn called the Eleven Cricketers. A three door frontage comes next, the centre door has the name "June Cottage".

After this is "The Old Bakery", dated 1664, tile-hung as is "Courtyard House" next door. These for many years the home and shop of Mr and Mrs Groom who ran one of two bakeries in the Village and one of the first premises in the Village to have a gas supply. Mrs Groom would sell tea and buns to cyclists passing through the Village when this road was a main thoroughfare. Mr Groom gave up the business after his wife died and it was taken over by Tom Smallwood, son of the other baker in the Village, becoming the Climax Bakery.

After this are five "Rocks Cottages" which were built by the Rock family. Last but by no means least of the group is "Stone House" built also by the Rock family in the mid 1800's. It has an Italianate style porch, literally the last thing you would expect to see at the end of a terrace like this. A short distance on stood Chelsfield Fire Station, a yellow painted shed which contained a hand-pump. The site can still be detected at the side of the road.

Opposite is "Gladsholme", a red brick detached house of c1952. It stands on the site of another called "Brynterion". In 1864 a lady called Sarah Anne Morgan inherited the home from her father. In 1878 she married German artist Heinrich Sigismund Uhlrich who came from Oschatz in Saxony. They were a well known and well liked couple in the Village but had to put up with some anti-German hysteria during W W 1. Sarah died in 1927 and Heinrich lived on in the house with his health in decline until he died in Farnborough Hospital on 5th November 1937. While he was in the hospital "Brynterion" burnt down. This was at the end of November 1936 so he was hospitalised for a considerable time. Arson was suspected and some thought it may have been because of his

German origin but it was later said that a couple of gipsies from the St Mary Cray area had been responsible. Although the Fire Station was just across the road it seems, at the time, there was no one available who knew how to use the hand-pump and by this period it was probably unserviceable anyway. By the time the regular fire brigade arrived it was too late. The site of the house lay derelict until after W W 1 when in was bought by the landlord of the Five Bells and the new house built. Uhlrich's work was mainly local views and portraits and only a few are known to survive. He signed his work with his initials H S U; keep checking out those boot sales.

The Five Bells was originally a farm house with about four acres which became an inn in about 1680. It was named Five Bells after the bells newly installed in the Church eight years earlier in 1672. It has been extended a number of times as can be seen by looking at the side wall from Warren Road. The pub serves good food. It was voted Pub of the Year in 2010 by CAMRA.

The large weatherboard building on the opposite corner is "Cross Hall". The earliest recorded date for it is 1612 but is considerably older possibly 550 years. The shop front thankfully still in place served a bakery run by Thomas and Annie Smallwood from 1882, not only selling from here but making deliveries to the surrounding area. One of their sons, George, a Private in the Border Regiment, was killed in action in the Great War on 26th October 1917 at the age of 26. Another son, Tom, followed his father into the baking business, first of all at Faversham and then moving back to the Village and taking over the Grooms premises. When Thomas retired in 1933 the two bakeries merged. It seems odd today that a small village could have two successful bakeries for so many years. Perhaps people ate a lot of bread in those days. Later "Cross Hall" became the headquarters of Bill and Dick Sanderson the local builders. The crest displayed in the front is that of the Suffolk Regiment in which Dick Sanderson served. There was at one time also a butchers in "Cross Hall" to the left of the bakers.

Next to "Cross Hall" on the corner of Church Road and Skibbs Lane, are some small modern houses. These replaced a row of ancient "Cross Hall" and "Ivy Cottages" demolished in 1960's when such things were not appreciated.

Around the corner in Warren Road is the stop for what is probably the Village's best friend, the R3 bus, providing a vital link with the rest of the, even in this day and age, seemingly different, world. Once the 407 terminated in the Village after coming down on what was the main road from Dartford through the Crays. Later it was replaced by the 477. Also later the 431 came here via Orpington. Now just the R3 stops here for a few minutes while the driver has a short break (if on time) before changing the destination sign from Chelsfield Village to Princess Royal Hospital. It then sets off on its ridiculously meandering route to its other terminus.

The stop is outside the Village School, the one attended by Miss Read. The first school was built here in 1823 when there were about 49 pupils. By the 1860's this number had trebled with children walking here from Green Street Green, Well Hill and Pratts Bottom; (how did they manage it without the 4X4 school run?). The existing school dates from 1864 and is by Joseph Clark.

In 1883 a schoolmaster was appointed by the name of William Elias Bailey. He became extremely popular and respected and was elected to the Parish Council. On 12th July 1906 he joined a group of firemen and tradesmen from Orpington and St Mary Cray on an outing to Brighton, hiring a double deck bus from Vanguard (absorbed by London General two years later). At Handcross Hill in Sussex the brakes failed. The driver attempted to slow down by putting the bus into reverse with disastrous results on the transmission. (In the unlikely event you find yourself in this position leave the vehicle in whatever forward gear it is in and use engine braking). The bus hit a tree and the wooden body disintegrated. Six people were killed instantly and four others died later from their injuries including Mr Bailey who being too poorly for the journey to hospital was taken to the Red Lion Inn where he died two days later. A large funeral was held at St Martin's. An even larger one took place at St. Mary Cray where one of the deceased was local undertaker Henry Hutchings. One of the injured was also a school teacher, Mr Robert Pugh, headmaster of Wellington Road School, Orpington, who sustained a broken thigh which troubled him for the rest of his life.

Across the road is the old Methodist Church of 1872. A Methodist meeting house was licensed at Pratts Bottom, then in Chelsfield parish, in 1810. In the upper part of the old parish, the first Methodist meeting was held in the kitchen of Hewitts Farmhouse and to commemorate it the date 16 Feb 1812 was scratched on a small pane of glass in the door. This is now displayed on the wall of the current Methodist Church in Windsor Drive. Between 1840 and 1872 meetings were held in a rented room at "Cross Hall". As well as the regular services Sunday School was also held at the church, sometimes conducted by Percival Bowen of Wheatsheaf Farm. When the new church was built in 1966 this one became a private dwelling.

Orlestone Gardens is built on the site of the 19th cent Rectory demolished in the 1960's. It was of an intermediate five bedroom size. "Rounds" is a newish house, in a mixture of styles, on the site of the one occupied by James Smith, builder and undertaker (an interesting combination) and the contractor responsible for maintenance work on the pump at Well Hill. In the front garden is Mr Smith's workshop painted white. John Round occupied this farm in Chelsfield in the 1770's, part of the Manor of Chelsfield. A footpath adjacent goes to Court Road opposite St. Martin's. Across Warren Road is "Little Lillys" built just post war by the Sandersons to replace another also destroyed by same V1 which hit Lillys. It has since been enlarged. The land was once part of the Lillys Farm estate.

The Chelsfield Village rail pond has recently had some much needed conservation work. Behind is a barn converted or rebuilt as residential accommodation. "Orchard Cottage" opposite is red brick with rendered upper floor. Originally a pair built in 1908 as gardeners cottages for Chelsfield House. "Harefield", a late Edwardian substantial detached villa, was designed by J. W. Rowley. This was another house used as temporary accommodation during and just after WW11.

Now turn back to Chelsfield Lane and you see the main entrance to Lillys Farm. Lillys Cottages were re-built post war by the Sandersons and designed by George Rose. The Farm has a plant nursery, a stoneware outlet and The Koi Water Barn.

Just up Chelsfield Lane is Lillys Farmhouse another Sanderson production contemporary with the cottages and of similar design but tile-hung. The old farmhouse was dated to the 16th cent. and stood here until the afternoon of 27th June 1944 when it was destroyed by a falling V1 missile. The tenants Mr Frederick Chapman, a former police constable and then on the reserve list, and his wife Edith were killed together with many of the dogs they bred for Sidcup Kennels. Two more were seriously injured but it was fortunately the kennel maid's day off so she escaped injury and was able to come back and tend the surviving dogs.

What brought the V1 down seems controversial. Two witnesses said it was tipped by a fighter over Well Hill. Others said a pilot fired at it and another source says it was probably brought down by a balloon. It could of course be a combination, the pilot firing at the V1 when he noticed the direction of its fall. Shooting down was not preferred as the detonation of the 1 ton of explosive carried endangered the attacking aircraft. A former Spitfire pilot that I spoke to stated that it was not the practice of his colleagues to tip so close to a built up area. So without the evidence of the pilot involved or his log I doubt if we will ever know.

If finishing your walk here it is only a short distance back to the Village centre.

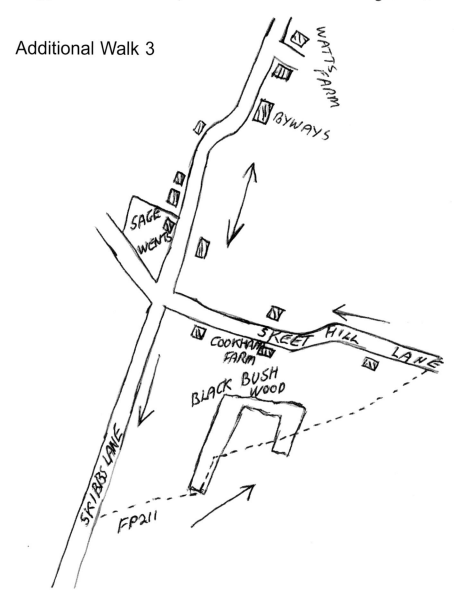

"Bucks Cross Cottages", 1 & 2, some of the oldest in Chelsfield.

The bad winter had damaged the hedge allowing this picture of the east side of the above.

The original entrance to "Chelsfield House".

The 407 bus ran to Chelsfield between 1925-1935. Here the driver tops up the radiator in the village. The water came from the Five Bells where it's said the crew topped up with something stronger. The bus is an AEC NS-type. They were originally built with solid tyres and later converted to pneumatics. This one has also gained wider domed front wings and improved lighting.

"Chelsfield House" looking impressive as the reception block for the Chelsfield Park Hospital.

The R3 bus leaves the village for Maypole and Bo-Peep before travelling to seemingly every part of Orpington to reach Princess Royal (University) Hospital, formerly Farnborough Hospital.

Late 40's picture of the village centre with Post Office on the right
and a row of old cottages opposite.

Main Street 1865. The nearest shop is Thompson's Store, later to become Neal's.
The picture was taken by Bromley photographer and music seller Robert Harman.

Mid terrace "The Old Bakery".

End of terrace "Stonehouse".

The village hall. The flag is still flown in Chelsfield. It's a good job somebody does.

"Cross House", the old post office.

3 & 4 Bucks Cross Cottages, formerly known as "Kidders", opened as the first school in the village in 1720. The attic room was used.

The village pond has had recent much needed conservation.
Behind is a barn conversion/rebuild and a garden phone box.

KENTISH TIMES, FRIDAY, DECEMBER 4, 1936.

:STROYED BY FIRE.—The Crystal Palace, Sydenham, was destroyed by
photograph was taken as the raging flames, fanned by a strong wind, wer:
n end to end of the building.

CHELSFIELD ARTIST'S BURNT-OUT HOME. — The remains
of the cottage of Mr. Heinrich Uhlrich, retired artist, of Chelsfield,
destroyed by fire early on Friday morning last. Mr. Uhlrich is at
present in Farnborough Hospital. He is 94 years of age and has no
relatives.

Mr Uhlrich's house burnt down just three days before the Crystal Palace but the latter got a larger
audience. The Crystal Palace is in Penge, not Sydenham!

"The Five Bells", still the centre of the village.

"Cross Hall". The shop front to the right was the baker's, later a builder's office, and the butcher's was to the left.

The old Methodist Church, now a private house.

The old forge in Skibbs Lane. To the left is the workshop where carts were made with the paint shop over. I am told the iron sheeting is original. To the right is the building where the horse shoeing was carried out. The shutter door is of course a later adaptation.

Before: Lilleys Farmhouse intact. (Geoffrey Copus collection)

After: The remains (from a different side). Despite taking a direct hit, a lot of the timber framing still stands. (Geoffrey Copus collection)

The coal post in Skibbs Lane.

The former Knox-Cummingham residence in Chelsfield Lane.

Around Goddington

A walk of 2 - 2½ miles

From the direction of the R3 bus stop walk into Chelsfield Lane past the rebuilt Lillys Farmhouse.

Lillys

After Peter Collett died in 1607 it was inherited by his daughter Dame Hester Awcher whose husband was Sir Antony Awcher. In 1617 the tenant James Stile bought half the property and his son also James came to own the remainder by the time he died in 1677. The death of his grandson James Styles in 1710 led to the acrimonious "Great Chelsfield Inheritance Case" of 1729-1733 which hinged on the existence or non-existence of a will which one cousin alleged another had wilfully destroyed. The story, like something out of a Dickens book makes an entertaining chapter in "Chelsfield Chronicles". At the end of the sorry affair Lillys was owned by cousin James Burton. In 1788 ownership of Lillys passed to Mary, wife of James Aynscomb, heir to the Goddington estate. A year earlier their daughter Mary had married James Harris. One of their sons John inherited the Farm and it was in the ownership of the Harris family until after WW11. John was the last of the family to farm the land himself and thereafter it was let, hence the Chapmans in occupation in 1944.

In 1907 Lillys was inherited by George St Pierre Harris (1853-1939) an architect of some note locally. He began working as an architect in 1876 and designed many projects in and around Orpington. Apart from those mentioned earlier Pratts Bottom School is another good example.

You now have a choice of two routes to reach Goddington Park. You can walk straight up Chelsfield Lane watching out for the traffic or take footpath FP208 on the left which goes across a field to the Park. When you reach it keep towards the right around playing fields in the area called Rounds Smallams until you come to the Park entrance from Chelsfield Lane. In the Spring you can look for bluebells on the way. In a Council committee meeting on 17th March 1939, "Attention was called to the damage done to the bluebells at Goddington Park in previous years, and the Committee Resolves, that notices be displayed ......warning the public against contravening the Councils Byclaws with respect to the plucking of flowers, etc; and indicating the amount of penalty payable on conviction." The groundsman was instructed to keep the matter under careful observation. On another meeting on 28th June it is reported that the groundsman has been sacked, probably not just for losing too many bluebells, but because his work was "not satisfactory". On appeal he was demoted to assistant groundsman at Poverest but had to vacate the Lodge at Goddington which had gone with the job there and was included in the wage of £2.10.00. per week.

On the opposite side of Chelsfield Lane to the Park entrance is Lillys Wood, at one time known as Wally Wood, which is a public area with a path around its perimeter which makes a pleasant walk. Until recently it was not too over-managed like some conservation areas but now some thinning out is taking place along the paths as it seems the "health and safety" brigade has infiltrated. An unmarked footpath at the top of the "loop" would take you to Skibbs Lane. A balloon brought down a V1 in the Wood on the 21st July 1944. The remains lay in the Wood for some years but have now gone. The area was once a popular playground for local children but nowadays they have to be taken to a specially constructed play area like the one in Goddington Park where the brightly-coloured apparatus are surrounded by forgiving surfaces so if they fall they can't hurt themselves.

At the entrance to Goddington Park is coal post inscribed 24VIC, the twenty-fourth year of the reign of Queen Victoria. The one in Skibbs Lane has a more accurate 24&25 CAP 42, twenty four years and twenty five days of the Queen's reign. CAP is for the Latin "capitulum" (charter) and 42, the number of the bill for that year. The Coal Tax began in 1666 to help fund rebuilding after the Great Fire. The London Coal and Wine Duties (Continuance) Act of 1861 redefined the boundary, corresponding to that of the Metropolitan Police District, at which duty was payable on goods entering London. Most posts were newly cast by Henry Grissell of the Regent's Canal Ironworks although some earlier markers were relocated. They were sometimes called "iron men". Other types included cast iron plates and short iron and tall stone obelisks, the nearest of the later is situated next to the railway line approaching the station at Swanley. It's related that the contractors started the installation work at Green Street Green and continued in a circle around London. When they got back they found they had some left over. Rather than "take them home" they planted the remainder along the main road there. The tax was scrapped in 1890 when duty was 1s 1d per ton of coal. I have always wondered how effectively the duty was collected; there can't have been a man at every marker to take it and there must have been considerable evasion. Perhaps it relied on the threat of penalties for enforcement.

The Council bought a strip of land in 1934 to make an entrance into Goddington Park from Chelsfield Lane.

The homes in this part of Chelsfield Lane date from the 20's on with one earlier exception. The third on the left is "Woodland Cottage", a white rendered house of no particular architectural merit. It was once the home of Sir Samuel Knox-Cunningham M.P. Born in Ireland he was educated in Edinburgh and Clare College Cambridge where he achieved a heavyweight Blue in boxing and became a fully qualified Amateur Boxing Association judge. He became M.P. for South Antrim and Personal Private Secretary to Harold MacMillan. He came to Chelsfield in the early 40's and gave financial assistance to Chelsfield Cricket Club and Well Hill Boys Club. Lady Knox-Cunningham was President of the All England Women's Institute. The couple both loved cats. Unfortunately, as we can determine, the traffic along this stretch of road does tend to speed a little and some of the Knox-Cunningham cats used up all of their nine lives here so their owners moved away to somewhere more pet friendly.

Allandale Place is a close of modern houses, "Homestead" is a good example of one of the earlier houses in the lane and "Holly Cottage" is the first built on this stretch of road, a nicely proportioned small home with tile-hung upper floor. Past Craven Road "Oakway" is a bungalow with curved roof-line and long half-moon attic. A G. R. post box is set into the gate post, painted black to show it is no longer public (but I wouldn't mind betting some people are still fooled). Dorado Gardens is a close of modern Georgian inspired houses.

Nut Tree Close of the 50's or 60's is on the approximate site of "Chang-ann-Tang", a house built between 1871 and 1897, and another house. Chang is a Chinese name but otherwise the phrase is apparently meaningless in the language. Broad Walk is another close of modern houses. Just past Avalon Road is another bungalow with a half-moon attic window. The homes on this side back onto Tripes Farm. There are no buildings of interest here but there are the Orpington Sale Rooms for auctions, a centre for health and fitness and some units dealing with bathroom fittings and blinds. The farmhouse with a barn (said to be 500 years old), converted to residential use and some modern units designed to match, are opposite the main farm entrance. The appearance of the farmhouse is deceiving as it is much older than it looks. The older part of the building can be glimpsed from Loxwood close. Just past the farm a footpath to the right is another section of the Chelsfield Circular. The road junction with Skeet Hill Lane marks the extent of Chelsfield here. Return to and enter Craven Road.

The Craven estate was developed from the late 1890's by architect William Albert Williams who later developed the Tower Road area of Orpington. Not much was built here until the 20's. Craven Road has a varied selection of homes the oldest of which, probably early 20th cent. are a pair at 44/46 and "Ivy Cottage" 42 which is slim and narrow with a tall shuttered window to the upper front. Hawfield Bank is a close of modern weatherboard houses.

At the end of Craven Road you emerge into Avalon Road. To the right are fairly recent homes of standard design. To the left is much the same apart from a few attractive but standard type semis of the late 30's by Goddington Estates Ltd. towards the low numbers. Gillmans Road on the north side next to the fire station echoes "Gillmans Brimstone". The fire station of the 60's may be replaced in the near future. The bus stops in Avalon Road are for the R9. All the other roads to the south of Avalon Road; Woodly Road, Lapworth Close, Pendennis Road and Close and the Berrylands estate are all modern housing. A few yards along Avalon Road, with the modern Burwood School opposite, take the footpath, left, back into Goddington Park.

The Manor of Goddington

The manor of Goddington is said to be named after Simon de Godynton who obtained it from the Crown in 1346 although the family may have been resident in the area for some time before this date. Edward 111 was into the 20th year of his reign and may have been giving out rewards at this time. After numerous changes of ownership and passing back and forth to Crown, it came into the possession of the James Styles of Lillys by 1706. Following the division of property to resolve the inheritance case mentioned above, Goddington eventually passed to Mary Aynscomb who married James Harris in 1787. This led to the bringing together the Goddington and Lillys estates back into common ownership. "Common", perhaps, isn't the right word to use here as when their daughter Maria chose to marry a Keston builder, William Cole in 1835, which James considered quite definitely below her station, he took steps to ensure only his three sons inherited, although he did make a small financial provision for her. One can well imagine the atmosphere at the family dining table after the impending union had been announced. The wedding took place in Lewisham which may tell us something. When the estate was divided between the sons, the eldest, James, got Goddington.

It would be useful to explain here that the law of Gavelkind applied in Kent and only in Kent, said to be one of the concessions made by William Duke of Normandy in 1066 on his way to Dover in exchange for the allegiance of the population. All sons equally inherited their father's land instead of the eldest in the rest of the Country. Any estate owner who wished his eldest son to succeed needed an Act of Parliament until Gavelkind was abolished in 1925.

The Manor remained in the Harris family until 1871 when after a brief period in other ownership was obtained by George Hallett, a businessman in Rotherhithe. He did not have long to enjoy his new home however as he died in 1873 with his wife Marianne passing soon after. Goddington then descended to Emily Caroline Hallett who just before her death in 1892 gave it to nephew Alexander Miller-Hallett. It was he who had "Goddington House" (built 1875) extensively remodelled in the 1890's by William West Neve. Three new lodges and the larger "Red Lodge" were also built in the grounds about this time. Mr. Miller-Hallett made many other changes in the Park grounds.

Before 1914 a good many servants were employed but the coming War would change much. One of Alexander and wife Amy's six children, son Stewart, a Second Lieutenant in the South Wales Borderers was killed at Mametz Wood in July 1916. In 1919 the estate was put up for auction but little if any was sold. Another was held in 1929 with much the same result. A third took place in 1931 and the house was sold at this time or soon after. Amy Miller-Hallett died in 1932 and is buried at St. Martin's but Alexander, the former last Lord of the Manor, lived on until 1953, dying at Rottingdean at the age of 97.

In 1934 Orpington Council purchased the parkland with a loan of £15,221 and the additional strip linking it with Chelsfield Lane for £1,300 with the intention of creating a public open space. For the first few months it was let for cattle grazing and not officially opened as a park until 1936. A dispute with the new owners of the house who had "accidentally" erected a fence on Council land was settled with an exchange of ground. In 1938/9 the Council received a grant of £200 from the National Playing Fields Association and £1,000 from the Carnegie United Kingdom Trust towards the cost of purchasing the ground. By 1947 additional land adjacent to Chelsfield Lane had been purchased from the Lillys estate (£5,685).

As you enter the Park ahead of you is a now little used pavilion constructed in 1939 for the Council by Kent Builders Ltd. along with others in parks and recreation grounds in the Borough. The original plans where altered to provide improved accommodation for use as a first-aid post in the event of war.. Earlier Mr Miller-Hallett had been a cricket enthusiast and was Chairman of the Cricket Club which took part in matches of some merit in the Park. He was also the founder of a ladies team. If you walk towards the right you can see "Goddington House" behind the trees. Walking over to this corner of the Park you will find a footpath which leads through to Court Road more or less parallel to the driveway to "Goddington House", now converted to flats and belonging to a housing association but still looking much as it did at the turn of the century in a sort of "arts and crafts" style. Beside the drive to your left is "Wayside Lodge" one of the three built c1895.

From the entrance to "Goddington House's" drive at Court Road you can look across to Park Avenue which before the bypass was the main drive to the House from Orpington. At the other end at Sevenoaks Road is another lodge, "Park Lodge", where the gate keeper lived. A pair of large iron gates closed the drive off to all but the invited. The gate keeper would almost certainly have other duties as just opening and closing a gate occasionally would be far too easy. Lodges were often used for guest accommodation and looking after these may well have been another task. "Park Lodge" is well kept with a neat wooden fence and well tended garden. It is a good 3/4 mile down Park Avenue and not a very exciting walk. most of the homes are standard types, chalet bungalows at the top and mock Tudor by the forest load for most of the rest. There are a few attractive houses among them including some 30's detached with wide curved entrance porches. All this area of the Park was developed from the thirties together with Gravelpit Farm up to Spur Road which also belonged to the Goddington estate. If you wish to go this way please follow additional walk 4. if not the best way to see "Park Lodge" is to go to the War Memorial at Orpington; all the buses stop there, and walk the short distance to Park Avenue two roads down. If you are feeling lazy you can see the lodge from the R3 bus as it heads towards Chelsfield Village. The only other thing of interest here is the nearby Methodist Church. The Methodists like their foundation stones which is useful if you want to date the building. The one on the front corner of the church is dated June 10th 1933. There are no less than 22 others, most undated and naming benefactors and mainly sited around the hall which is slightly later in a different art deco style.

Additional walk 4
About 1½ miles

From Court Road walk down Park Avenue. As you go down you pass an entrance to the playing field of St Olaves School who re-located here from London many years ago. Most of the more attractive houses are towards the lower reaches of Park Avenue. At the end of this road you see "Park Lodge" on the corner of Sevenoaks Road. Turn right to find the Methodist Church on the next corner. Turn right again and up Hillcrest Road. Nearly all the homes are standard semis getting newer as you go. Between 76 and 78 a footpath leads through back to Park Avenue A short distance down this road another path beside the school plying field goes to Goddington Lane. Here are good houses of the 20's and 30's. Turn left and past Warwick Close and you will see another coal post bearing the fuller length inscription. Pass Durley Gardens (which echoes Durley's Lane), and Goddington Chase. On the corner of Dene Drive at 61 Goddington Lane is "Red Lodge", dated 1898, built for the Goddington estate and resembling a larger version of the park lodges. On the opposite side of the road are two complementary houses, one a few years later and one new. At the top of Goddington Lane turn left into Court Road to reach Park Avenue.

The stretch of Court Road at Goddington is mostly 30's and 40's houses and bungalows. The most interesting group is conveniently adjacent to the Park entrance here. "Wayside Lodge", looking a bit sad at present is 301, 303 and 305 are a couple of detached houses, 307 has gone, replaced by a new Asprey Homes development, Hurstlands Drive, which backs onto the Park and seems to have just "crept in" before the garden building ban, 309 is one of the larger detached houses with double-fronted ground floor and 311 is a quite attractive and well proportioned three story modernist house with a sun lounge at the top.

Return into the Park and proceed in an anti-clockwise direction. War fever was beginning in 1937 and the park was used for exercises by the 65th Brigade Royal Artillery which afterwards brought complaints of damage to nearby footpaths. Air raid precaution talks began in Orpington about this time. In 1944 part of the Park was requisitioned by the R.A.F. Balloon Section in response to the flying bomb attacks.

You pass the Bowling Club to reach the third of the lodges, "Goddington Park Cottage", which would probably have guarded the tradesmen's entrance during the estate days and was used as a ground-keepers cottage after the public park was decided upon. There is a car park (free) off Goddington Lane. In 1773 James Aynscomb had the Lane diverted from its previous route which passed along on the far side of what is now the bypass. Before Court Road it was the main road between Orpington and Chelsfield. It now ends abruptly after looping across Court Road and back to it. It is not known why Mr Aynscomb wanted the road brought closer to his house as he seems at odds with his contemporaries almost all of whom preferred to keep the Great Unwashed as far from their place of residence as possible. It seems ironic now that the bypass eventually came very close indeed.

Straight on from here are standard bungalows, (this small estate of bungalows was developed in the late 30's by Loxley Builders). Go right here to Court Road. On the opposite side of Court Road is a range of useful retail outlets which at the time of writing are two convenience stores, one a newsagent, a cafe, a fish and chip shop, an off licence, a butchers , a filling station which also sells refreshments and has a customer toilet, a ladies hairdresser, a car rental office and a Volvo dealership. The first shops here were erected c1936/7, of which a couple remain now as one unit, about the same time as the first filling station was opened on the corner of Goddington

Lane. Charterhouse Road, has R3 bus stops. From here walk down Court Road in a south easterly direction, the right hand side is best. The blocks of 60' or 70's flats on this side is Saltwood Close. On the left a bungalow has been replaced with two new houses which are unlike any other property in the road and appear out of place at present. They may soon be joined by a third new house on a smaller plot adjacent.

After passing the final end of Goddington Lane on the left, Westcombe Park and Orpington Sports Club (established late 30's), is home to Westcombe Park Rugby Club, Orpington Cricket Club, Nomads Women's Cricket Club, Orpington Football Club, Orpington Tennis Club and Orpington Table Tennis Club.

You pass the end of The Highway down which the Church Parish boundary runs. At the other end is Warren Road and Chelsfield Station. There is another R3 bus stop here in Court Road. Most of the homes are modern (50's on) with some pairs of older semis and bungalows towards the Court Road end,(some by Morrell c1937 and a bit later by H. C. Richardson and H. Miller). There is also The Highway School built in c1950 to serve this developing area. The classrooms were of a prefabricated construction using aluminium members from the Second World War aircraft industry. The architecture was therefore not great. Rebuilding work is now being undertaken; the central part being retained with the wings replaced by new classrooms by architect Stefan Pop. The front gates are of note incorporating figures of children and animals into the ironwork. These were designed by Chris Ploughman of Romsey Hants. The R1 bus stops here.

Continuing down Court Road a parallel service road runs for a short distance fronting post bypass homes mostly from the late 30's in various styles including a pair of bungalows with small half-moon attic windows. This length of road is probably a cross section of the homes built in this area just prior to and just after WW11. The landscape then turns to fields until you reach Warren Road. Just before the road on the right is a footpath and a bridleway both of which run almost parallel to Warren Road as far as Chelsfield Station. On the opposite side of Court Road a path leads to the Village centre. Just around the corner into Warren Road is another pair of Mr Waring's 1860's cottages, "Warren Cottage" and "Anneth Lowen". On the other side is the red brick "Rose Cottage" showing some alteration. It was built in the 1870's as a lodge to "Court Lodge". Down Court Road again brings you to Church Road. Just before is a path to the Churchyard. An R3 bus can be caught nearby in the Village but you should not leave now as the best is yet to come.

Around Goddington

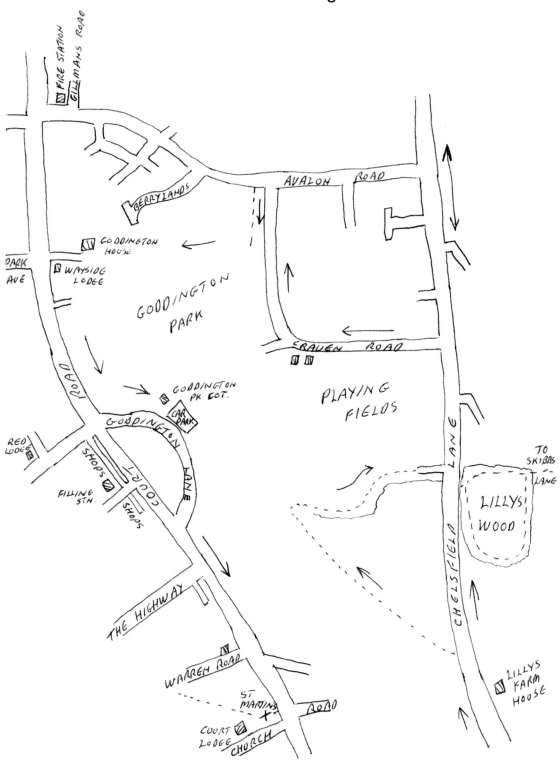

Additional Walk 4

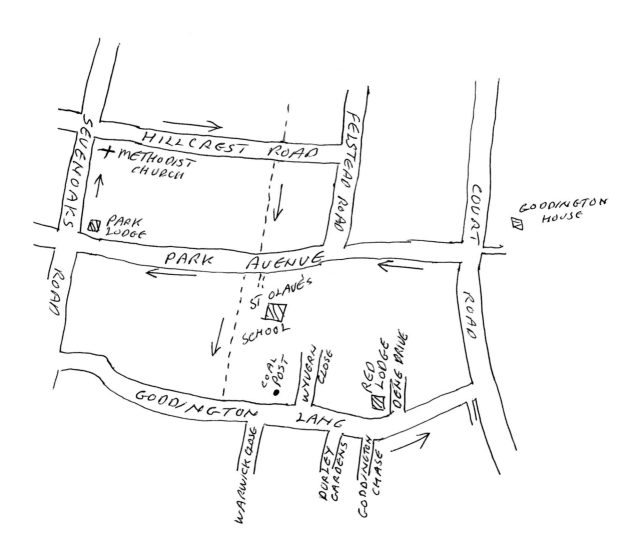

"Park Lodge" at the end of Park Avenue was the gatekeeper's house for Goddington.

Appearances can be deceptive. From Chelsfield Lane, Tripes Farmhouse looks fairly recent but behind is a very old building. The old barn can also be seen to the right.

"Goddington House" viewed from the park. It is a winter scene, the house being less visible when the trees are in foliage.

The pavillion in the park built in 1939.

Looking from the drive of "Goddington House" towards Park Avenue which was once its continuation.

The oldest group of houses in Craven Road.

"Red Lodge" in Goddington Lane.

Drawing by Randolph Caldecott showing Mr Brind and two of his children in the Churchyard with Court Lodge behind. From "Owls of Olynn Belfry", 1885. (Geoffrey Copus collection)

Court Lodge and St Martin's

A short walk

Hardly a walk at all but there is so much history here that it deserves a whole chapter. There are usually strong connections between a Manor house and the village church and it is indeed the case here.

Court Lodge

The building is difficult to see from the road but you can get a glimpse of it from the Churchyard. Adjacent is "Lodge House", c1860 and converted from outbuildings. Court Lodge is a large house of two storeys plus attic and dating from c1700 in its present form although parts are thought to be older. At Church Road is an early 20th cent lodge. The Court Lodge gets its name from the Courts Baron which were held to set and collect rents and deal with other matters connected with the running of the Manor.

    The track to Court Lodge has no Public Right of Way. The residents are not happy about members of the public walking up this private access and they ask that their privacy be respected.

The Manor of Chelsfield to 1771

The origins of the Manor go back well before the conquest when it was part of Godwin's holdings, but was not known as a Manor because Manor is a Norman word meaning "land belonging to a man of honour". The first Norman owner of Chelsfield however did not quite live up to this description. It was one of about a hundred Manors in Kent and a good number elsewhere given to Odo, Bishop of Bayeux, half brother of William 1, who also created him Earl of Kent (one source calculates his total holding at 439 manors). You would think that this would be more than enough for him but not so and he soon began to appropriate land belonging the Church including part of Bromley Manor. In 1076 Lanfranc, Archbishop of Canterbury, took Odo before the "shire mote" on Penenden Heath and after a trial lasting three days, 25 Manors, or parts there of, in various counties were returned to the Church. By 1084 William had had enough of Odo, deprived him of his Earldom and had him imprisoned at Rouen. After the death of William 1 Odo returned but was soon in conflict with William 11 and finally lost all his English possessions and was banished, dying in 1096.

A full list of the Manor's owners would make tedious reading so I will just mention some of the more prominent. The de Chelsfield family held it in the 12th and 13th centuries, Simon de Chelsfield was for a time Sheriff of Kent. It was the property of Simon de Montfort until he lost it, and his life, in a rebellion in 1264. Otho de Grandison was owner from 1289 to 1358. Rare among the early owners of the Manor he liked and took an interest in Chelsfield. The Earl of Wiltshire owned it from 1406 but was beheaded in 1461. Robert Poynings died childless in 1470 and the Manor returned to the Crown until the reign of Elizabeth 1 when the Walsinghams held it for two generations before it passed to the Giles family.

In 1657 the Manor was acquired by Thomas Norton. He was succeeded by his son called Gravely, which was his grandmother's surname. It was in the time of his son another Thomas Norton that the current house was built probably based on the older building. He died in 1749 and having on children left the estate to his sister-in-law's son Henry Martin who ten years later sold it to James Maud, a City wine merchant. James lived at Gatton in Surrey and when he died in 1769 his only child Mary inherited the Court Lodge estate. In 1771 Mary married Brass Crosby.

Brass Crosby

Brass Crosby whose blue plaque can be seen here was born on 8th May 1725 in Stockton-on-Tees. He was christened Brass as this was his mother's maiden which his parents wished continue into the next generation. He went to the City of London with little money to practice law and did quite well for himself with this and other ventures. Marrying twice to women in a better financial position than he must have helped. He became member for Tower Ward in 1758, Alderman of Bread Street Ward in 1765 and M.P. for Honiton in 1768. 1770 saw Crosby become Lord Mayor of London. Upon acceptance of the post he declared that at the risk of his life he would protect the liberties of the citizens of London.

While Crosby was acting as Chief Magistrate together with fellow magistrates Alderman Oliver and John Wilkes, printers were brought before them on three occasions charged with breach of privilege because they reported debates in Parliament. Each time the Magistrates rejected the case as invalid. M.P.s (who at this time had even more to hide than they do now), were furious and sent Crosby and Alderman Oliver, (Wilkes was not brought to the bar on a technicality), to the Tower. They spent about six weeks there and were released when the Speaker's writ ran out at the end of the session, riding back to Mansion House in a procession of 53 carriages. No one was ever prosecuted for reporting debates again. Out of this would come the publication of "Hansard" and from Brass Crosby's actions comes the saying "bold as Brass".

Crosby had known Mary for some time being a friend of her father, (who no doubt supplied him with a few bottles of wine at a good price), but she did not want to marry him while he was Lord Mayor as she preferred a more low profile existence. When he left office she became his third wife. For six months of the year they would live here at Chelsfield and for six months at their London home at Chatham Place. Brass died at the London address on 14th February 1793. The hearse was driven 16 miles through Lewisham to Chelsfield for the biggest funeral the Village has ever seen. An obelisk monument was erected in St George's Circus, Blackfriars. In 1905 it was moved to the grounds of Bethlem Royal Hospital of which Crosby had become president in 1782. The building is now the Imperial War Museum. Mary died on the 5th October 1800.

Having no children Mary willed the estate to her cousins George and Francis Morland. George bought out Francis securing the whole for himself. He was an officer in the Earl of Albermarle's Dragoons. He had been partly educated in Paris and is said to have returned there after the revolution and bought Marie Antoinette's candlesticks. He and his wife Frances were childless and after he died in 1814 and his wife in 1817 the estate was passed to niece Elizabeth and her husband Robert Crawford. Mr. Crawford was not very good at running the estate. He several times raised loans by way of mortgage but in 1844 he gave up and put the property in auction. Failing to sell this way it was, a while later, bought by Thomas Waring.

Court Lodge, farm land and farm buildings were now let to tenant farmers and in 1857 when in the possession of a Mr. Bartholomew Spain a fire destroyed most of the outbuildings. Arson was suspected but no one apprehended. Soon after the retirement of the tenant William Waring took the decision to build a new Court Lodge Farmhouse and let the Court Lodge and a little surrounding land to the well-heeled. It proved to be a wise move.

The family of John Gordon, a barrister, were followed by the Brinds in about 1875.

Frederick William Brind was a wine merchant whose daughter Marian Harriet married Randolph Caldecott on March 18th 1880 at the church next door. Caldecott (1846-1886) is best known as an illustrator of children's books. He published two a year for the last ten years of his life some of them based on Chelsfield with characters inspired by real people of the Village. There is no plaque for him here but there is one at 46, Great Russell Street, Bloomsbury WC2, where he lived after leaving Manchester. Since 1938 the Caldecott Medal has been awarded annually to the best American artist-illustrator of Children's books.

When the Brinds left in 1892 the Lodge was let to George Edward Asprey and his family. Edward was the son of Charles Asprey II of Caterham, Surrey, and chairman of the famous Bond Street firm founded in 1781 by William Asprey, a descendent of Huguenots who had settled in Mitcham. George's first wife Caroline had died in 1888 and in 1892 he married his second wife Florence Caroline Rolls (another good name). His father died in this same year and these two events may have prompted his move to Chelsfield. He became Chairman of the company in 1909.

At Chelsfield the family suffered three major tragedies. Daughter Joan Rolls Asprey died of illness aged 10 in 1907, son Maurice, a Captain in the Buffs was killed in 1916 and Edward Asprey himself collapsed and died during a fire in 1918 while attempting to assist his chauffeur removing cars from the garage. Soon after the remaining family left.

Members of the Coutts family lived at Court Lodge from the 20's for a long period but as far as I know, none had any apparent connection with the bank of the same name.

Court Lodge, perhaps c1950. (Geoffrey Copus collection)

The old plough, grounded in love and St Martin's car park.

St Martin of Tours

There was almost certainly a Saxon church on or near the site of this one, although not mentioned in the Domesday Book, the compilers of which were not obligated to mention churches and mostly did not, even though there were many thousands. A church at Chelsfield appears in Textus Roffensis (c1115), itself probably a copy of an earlier document and is generally accepted as proof that a pre-conquest building existed. The one here now is basically Norman. No trace has been found of the earlier one but as it would probably have been mostly constructed of timber and any stone reused, it is unlikely that anything is left.

The church is dedicated to St. Martin of Tours although it has been erroneously shown on maps from time to time as St. Mary's or St. Margaret's. As related in the Church guide, Martin was born in Sabaria, Pannonia, now Hungary in 316. When he was 15 he was conscripted into the Roman Army. Five years later he shared his cloak with a beggar, cutting it in two with his sword and giving one half away. Martin afterwards had a vision of Christ wearing the cloak and as a result became a Christian and left the Army. In 361 he founded a community at Liguge and ten years later was elected Bishop of Tours. He died at Candes in 397 on 11th November which might seem appropriate now as he is the patron Saint of soldiers. It is not known if Martin ever came to England but his followers certainly did. They may have had a part in the conversion to Christianity of the owner of Lullingstone villa sometime between 364 and 378. Both Chelsfield and Eynsford churches which are close to the former entrances to the estate are dedicated to St. Martin. In 396 his friend Victricius, Bishop of Rouen came to this country because there was some concern among the French communities as to the slow expansion of the Church in Britain. St. Martin is often erroneously depicted in medieval armour when he of course wore standard Roman military apparel.

The oldest part of the church is that of the chancel and east end of the nave area, dated between 1080 and 1100. The nave was considerably lengthened a few years after. A narrow arch separated the chancel and nave. In the 13th cent. the chancel east wall was rebuilt with new windows, a chapel to the north, (which later became dilapidated and was removed), tower to the north and St. John's chapel to the south were all added. The porch dates from the 14th cent and the castellated upper section was added in the 18th cent.

In the Middle Ages the interior church walls were covered with brightly coloured illustrations. Few of these have survived in English churches but other denominations like the Greek Orthodox still paint their walls this way and a visit to one of these churches can give you an idea of how English churches once looked.

When the Reformation came no one stepped forward as a Martyr in Chelsfield. A document was signed in 1534 by the clergy of West Kent, with curate Thomas Glayve representing Chelsfield, renouncing the authority of the Pope and Rector Thomas Bacon adjusted his services to fit the new order and reworked them again when Mary came to the throne, dying the same year as the Queen (1558). The Vicar of Bray was the norm rather than the exception. Most people couldn't understand what it was all about and just got on with their lives.

Between 1649 and 1660 the Puritans held sway bringing in severe penalties for anyone found to be enjoying themselves and from 1653 banning the Clergy from officiating at marriage services. The church building suffered damage and neglect which had to be put right after the Restoration.

In 1672 five bells were cast by John Hodson of London, replacing, and possibly using the metal of, the three bells that were there from at least 1552. The bells were each inscribed "John Hodson Made Me 1672" together with the names of the churchwardens at the time and impressions of coins of the realm. They also bear the initials C H, thought to refer to Christopher Hodson who assisted, and later set up on his own at St. Mary Cray. The Hodsons also made cannons for the Navy and are said to have used iron ore dug out at Kevington. In 1880 the bells were re-hung in a new wooden frame by Gillett and Bland of Croydon. In 1936 a sixth treble was added, cast by Mears and Stainbank of Whitechapel. In 2009 the latter bell was sold to Nunney parish church, Somerset, and three new trebles cast by Taylors, Eayre and Smith of Loughborough to match the other five. Unusually, although dated 2008, they were not cast until 2009 the year of their dedication.

1857 saw "restoration" work carried out to the plans of Edwin Nash. Part of this work involved the removal of the Norman arch between the chancel and nave which some now criticize, but at the time was well received. The mid-1800's was not the time of conservation and Nash's idea was to create space which is what he did. Edwin Nash, who came from Farningham was a prolific church architect, unrelated to the famous John Nash but first cousin of William Waring which may have helped him get this job. His other local work includes a new church at St. John's, Penge (1849) with John Nash Round, in nearby Maple Road the St. Johns Cottages (1863), St. James', North Cray (1852) and All Souls, Crockenhill together with the vicarage and alms houses (c1856). St. Martin's Church interior was further opened up in 1896 when the ceiling was removed from the nave to once again expose the wonderful roof beams.

St. Martin's was damaged in 1944 when Lillys farmhouse was destroyed and Church windows were shattered. In 2006 the Brass Crosby extension, containing modern amenities, was opened.

Inside the Church

Walking up from the road to the top end of the car park you will find an old conventional drawn plough, with a notice inscribed "Rooted and Grounded In Love", presented by Marion Mills in memory of her husband Norman, a local farmer a short time after his death in 1991. The plough came from their farm and was often taken into church at harvest time.

In the porch is the War Memorial plaque erected by Rev. Norman Woodhall in 1951. Among the names you will see some I have mentioned on this walk; George Smallwood, Stewart Miller-Hallett, Maurice Asprey and the Chapmans. As with the vast majority of such memorials the list for WWI is much longer than for WWII showing that the effect on the average family in Britain during the Great War was more devastating than the following conflict despite the greater overall death toll. Having said that all wars are an abomination. I'm sure all those remembered here gave their lives with gallantry but they should not have had to. How was it that a handful of people high on ambition and low on common sense were allowed to cause such catastrophes? Why did so many follow them and why did so many cheer as they marched off? Most disturbing of all, why do, as recent history shows, such avoidable conflicts still continue? Some may think my comments here are an intrusion but I cannot with any conscience pass this memorial without condemning the events which led to the demise of those commemorated.

To enter the Church pull the door towards you and press down on the latch. You will find a light switch on your right. Inside you find an aura only found in an old English church. Always cool on the hottest of Summer days and to my mind never too cold in Winter but not everyone agrees on this point. A place of peace and tranquillity, almost a different world from the troubled one outside. Although I am not a regular church-goer I always feel welcome here as if this is a place I was meant to come to, the only one there sometimes, but never having a sense of being alone. I first came here as a youngster when my aunt Win was here arranging flowers, I think for Harvest Festival, and I thought then how light and uncluttered it looked compared with the church I had been to before with its acres of dark Gothic timber, (This was Holy Trinity, Beckenham, Lennard Road, in 1993 gutted by fire and restored using light colour timber which has made all the difference).

Going around the Church in a clockwise direction a window with plain glass is followed by a modern stained glass baptistry window. It was made by Maile of Canterbury; their armour device logo is incorporated in the window; and it is in memory of Jane Baker, a musician and wife of Lancelot Baker for a while assistant curate of this parish. Both worked at Cannock School. It is also in memory of B'Anne (Betty Anne) Baker (unrelated) and husband Ron who at one time lived at Lodge House. Both families were very loyal church goers and B'Anne made the pottery cross and candlesticks for the High Altar which can be seen here on weekdays. Mary with the infant Jesus is on the left side of the window and Joseph with cross its the right.

The font of octagonal shape, probably 17th cent, came from St. Paulinus Cray made redundant by the C of E in 1994 but is now happily back in use as a place of Worship as The Redeemed Christian Church of His Majesty House of Orpington (The House of Hope and Gods Wonder. Est. 2003), for which we give thanks. The font replaces a modern wood and stainless steel one which was not long fit for purpose and that in turn replaced one of stone which had crumbled. A metal insert, (made by Michael Murray), for the current one is only in place during use.

High up on the west wall, above the west door, is a circular window with a dove and below a larger window depicting St. Faith, patron saint of prisoners. These are in memory of Joan Asprey. A pair of windows, one each side, are now blocked. The wooden wall panelling was made by Mr Chapman of Seal in 1971. There is a memorial above the door which leads to the Brass Crosby extension. It is for Captain John Browne of Mile End in the parish of Stepney whose family owned a farm in Chelsfield. In the naming ceremony for the extension on 29th April 2007, a time capsule was placed in a hole in the wall here by Rt. Rev Dr. Brian Castle, Bishop of Tonbridge. The capsule was prepared by members of the church and contains various services in use today (showing that the Prayer Book is still in use), an article about the Rector and various pieces about life in the church and village. The pews are Victorian and made by the French family of Well Hill. An inscription under one reads "May 26th 1886, Arthur French".

A plain glazed window is followed by a memorial plaque to the members of the Asprey family who died while their home was at Chelsfield, a plaque to Joseph Baddeley, Rector 1898-1920 and memorial plaque for George Morland. Opposite the entrance door is a window showing St Michael and the angels fighting the devil disguised as a dragon. This is in to the memory of Stewart Miller-Hallett and was presented in 1920.

Don't forget to look up at the roof where the full crown post construction can be seen. The word "Nave" comes from a Latin word "navis" for ship and as you can see the roof looks like an upturned vessel.

The next memorial plaque is to the Burtons, James, Susanah and their son James of Lillys. After a plain window and the large memorial to Brass Crosby comes the tower arch at the base of the 13th cent. addition. The balustrade, in memory of Sidney Manger, and the ringing chamber were added in 1963. The screen was originally across the chancel before the Norman arch was removed in 1857. The pulpit with a carving of St. Martin dates from the 1970's. The Lectern was made by Tom Blatcher snr as was the Altar rail in St John's Chapel.

The organ presented by Mr. Miller-Hallett has a plaque to Miss Emily Caroline Hallett of Goddington dated 1893. There is a door to the vestry, which is on the site of the old north chapel demolished by the early 19th cent, and a squint window which enabled those in the chapel to see the High Altar. On the wall nearby is the image of a priest whose name is no longer known but was most likely a Rector of the parish. The Altar rail is 17th cent but not put in the Church until 1931, replacing a brass one.

We are now in the Sanctuary, in the oldest part of the Church. On the wall is a list of all the known Rectors. The most notable names are the three George Smiths, the first taking up office in 1576, and continuing through to the death of his grandson 74 years later in 1650. There is a small plaque to Canon Herbert William Mackay, Rector from 1938 to 1950 and the arched and recessed tomb of Robert de Brun, Rector, who died in 1417. There is a plaque to Dr. John Sandford, Rector 1774-1781 (d. 17th July 1781) and his widow Martha (d. 27th Oct 1798). Canon Leslie Virgo has recently retired after 37 years of dedicated service from 1974. From this date he also became the first Diocesan Adviser in Pastoral Care and Counselling for the Diocese of Rochester. For his work in this field, the protection of children and parish duties he was made Honorary Canon of Rochester Cathedral in 1983.

Lower down the wall a notice tells us about the lancet windows in the east wall, designed by Moira Forsyth to replace the Victorian ones damaged in 1944. The central parts of the windows containing the design were broken, and the replacement windows have nearly full length designs as seen. The old ones showed Christ crucified and the present, very appropriately Christ risen. They were paid for by public subscription together with a gift from the Coulthust Trust, founded by John William Coulthust of Skipton, and installed in 1951.

There are two stained glass windows in the south wall of the chancel. In one pair by Christopher Whall one shows St. Martin sharing his cloak and the other shows Christ receiving it. The window is a memorial to George Norman (d.1923), the grasshopper emblem being the logo of Martin's Bank. The stonework is in the style of Early English Geometric period. High on the wall above this window is a framed surviving section of the Victorian wall painting. Another pair of windows, by Christopher's daughter Veronica, show Christ and a kneeling knight. Christ has as his symbol the red cross the attribute of the risen Christ, (Christ is sometimes mistaken for St. George here). The stonework here is Perpendicular period style. The family tomb for the three George Smiths was placed here in 1651 by their surviving relatives. A plaque with its Latin inscription is above. There is another small Latin plaque on the wall before the door to the Churchyard to John Kynge (Kyng), Rector of Chelsfield 1420-1432. There is a brass plaque for Mary, wife of Edward Norman of Chelsfield House. The tapestry choir cushions and kneelers are by the Chelsfield Tapestry Guild in the 1960's. The Ten Commandments on the end of the nave wall and on the opposite side near the organ are Victorian.

You now come to what I think is the best part of the whole Church interior, St. John's Chapel. The focal point is the Peter Collett memorial. Two kneeling painted alabaster figures of Collett and his wife in prayer with two daughters behind her. Below two small infants lie on skulls. One of the daughters grew up to marry Peter Heyman and she was the mother of the little child lying alone on the wall in a prim bodice and skirt, leaning her head on an elbow. The east window of the chapel has two stained glass shields, one of All Souls College Oxford, patrons of the living since 1753 and the other of Sir Otho de Grandison, of the patron family from about 1219. If Sir Otho had died near Chelsfield he would have liked to have been buried here, but he died at Exeter in 1358 and is buried at Ottery St. Mary in a tomb with effigies of himself and his wife. Three stones in the floor under the window are for Gravely Norton and relatives Nicholas Huges (Hughs) and Thomas and Mary Fothergill. There is a small plaque to John Desmond Needham R.N. 26.9.42 A bas relief showing "The Annunciation" is in memory of Rev. John Ellingham, who as stated on the plaque below was Priest, Schoolmaster and Friend, Restorer of this Chapel 1892-1975. On a pillar at eye level you can see a small incised cross which may have been made for chapel consecration in the 13th century. The lancet window shows St. John, by Moira Forsyth, and is in memory of John Needham. The chapel screen was installed in 1948 at the suggestion of Rev. Ellingham.

Finally as we approach the porch door again is a large memorial plaque to James Maud, July 19th 1769, erected by daughter Mary Crosby.

The Brass Crosby room hosts coffee mornings and other events the details of which can be found in the Parish Magazine copies being available in the Church. A coin box is on the wall by the main door. Items are often sold at events including "Chelsfield" branded honey. Before leaving I think we must congratulate the members of St. Martin's for the immaculate way in which this church is kept.

The Churchyard

Coming out of the Church turn right to the west end. On the corner of the path on the ground to the left is a memorial (1) to the 126 whose remains were moved during the construction of the Brass Crosby extension. Looking up above the west door you will see the two blocked windows either side of St. Faith (2). The boundary wall was built in 1774 and has recently been restored.

Returning past the entrance porch immediately to the left is a horizontal gravestone with cross for George Hallett, his wife Marianne and his sister Emily Caroline (3). A door to the Chancel in the south wall has a recess adjacent which is a Holy Water Stoup (or stoop) (4). Blessed water would be placed here for people to cross themselves before entering the church. This door was originally the Priest's door but was subsequently used by others. Turning to the left you come to some of the Waring family graves, a large coffin-like tomb for Thomas and Sarah and also five of their children, flanked the graves of two others (5). Dr. Tarleton lies nearby under one of the flat ivy-covered tombs (6).

You come to a rough path that leads east down the lower graveyard. There is a memorial wall, used for the internment of ashes and now full (7). Some WW1 war graves include one of P. H. Thorpe of "H. M. S. Tyne" (d. 22/05/17) (8). This was the 4th H.M.S. Tyne launched in 1878 as the "S.S. Mariotis" for the Moss Line and later purchased by the Navy as a troopship and store carrier. It was sunk in 1920. Other war graves are to be found in all parts of the churchyard. To the right of the path towards the lower end is the Smallwood grave together with a note to the memory of George William whose remains are scattered somewhere in France (9).

Going back to the main churchyard and turning north you reach a junction of paths. The one ahead goes past a brick store to a gate and path to Court Road; the other heads west. By the gate are the remains of past fonts which should always be smashed to prevent their use as bird baths or other unseemly applications! (11). In the ground on this corner is an iron plaque to George Martin 1906 (10). Along by the churchyard wall are placed old fallen gravestones (12). Taking the westward path you come a horizontal stone with cross for Rev. Folliott Baugh (aged 80)and his wife(41) (13). Also here are some more of the Waring family, including William, Mary Wall, Arthur Thomas and William Arthur, two members of the Coutts family and Amy Miller-Hallett noting that she was the mother of Stewart Miller-Hallett. A large Celtic cross is on a Norman family tomb and to the left of this lay the Aspreys with an inscription which includes Maurice, buried abroad. (14). Further up the path you come to Percival Bowen and his wife and James Smith (15).

Turn left at the boundary wall of Court Lodge and to the left you will see an unusual stone in the shape of a Celtic cross within a frame (16). A rough easterly path beside the church leads to the eastern end of the Brass Crosby extension and opposite is a large coffin-type Harris family tomb (17).

The Churchyard

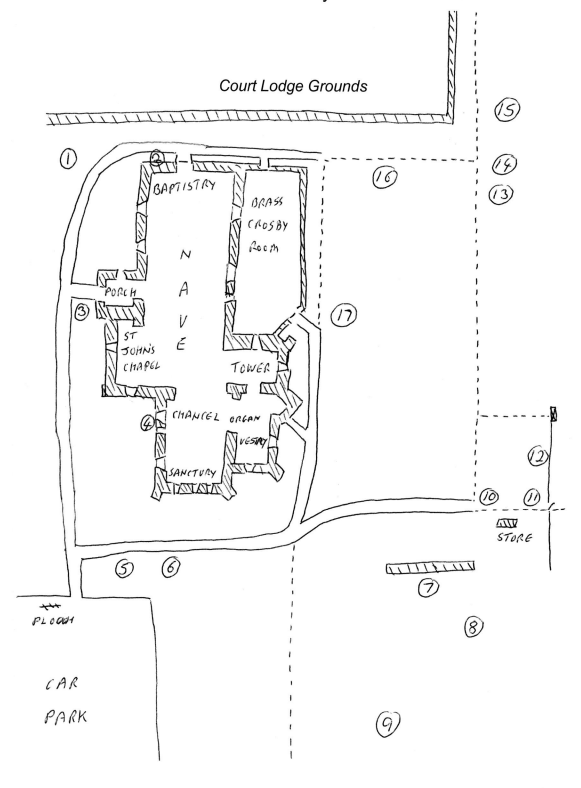

Court Lodge Grounds

St Martin's looking its best (it rarely looks otherwise) on a nice sunny day.

The show piece of St John's chapel, the Collett memorial.

The window that tells the story. On the left St Martin divides his cloak to give half away.
On the right is St Martin's vision of Christ receiving the cloak.

The church in 1900. The Brass Crosby extension is now against the wall to the right in this picture (west in church terms).

The tombs of Thomas and Sarah Waring and some of their children.

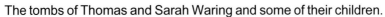

Tomb of George Hallett, wife Marianne and daughter Caroline. This and some other tombs in the churchyard had railings until a post WWII (which they survived) period of non-preservation when they were removed.

Unusual iron memorial to George Martin.

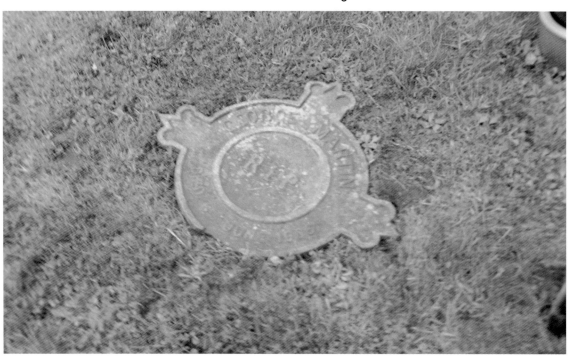

Railway related baptisms, marriages and burials
from Chelsfield parish registers 1864-1868

Baptisms

1864, 7th May, John George, son of John, railway labourer, and Elizabeth Skeels of Pratts Bottom, (buried 24th July).

1864, 12th June, William Abraham, son of William Henry, railway labourer, and Mary Elizabeth Osborne.

1864, 10th July, Thomas, son of Charles, railway labourer, and Caroline Horne of Green Street Green.

1864, 14th August, Thomas, son of Edward, railway labourer, and Jane Giles of Pratts Bottom.

1864, 9th October, Henry John, son of Thomas, railway contractor, and Mary Elizabeth Lansbury.

1865, 14th April, Emma, daughter of Daniel, railway labourer, and Mary Dodd of Railway Huts, Chelsfield (died 20th April aged 3).

1865, 9th July, Phoebe, daughter of Daniel, railway labourer, and Mary Dodd of Railway Huts, Chelsfield.

1865, 13th September, Beatrice, daughter of Thomas, railway labourer, and Mary Anne Lambert of Pratts Bottom.

1866, 9th May, Robert, son of John, railway labourer, and Agnes Barclay of Railway Huts, Chelsfield, (buried 20th May)

1866, 10th June, Sarah Beatrice Mary, daughter of George, railway labourer, and Frances Mead of Railway Huts, Broke Gate, Chelsfield.

1866, 10th June, Fanny, daughter of Joseph, railway labourer, and Sarah Anne Bray of Pratts Bottom.

1866, 10th June, Janet, daughter of John, railway labourer, and Agnes Barclay of Railway Huts, Chelsfield.

1866, 10th November, Frederick James, son of Thomas, railway contractor, and Mary Lansbury.

1867, 23rd May, John William, son of William, railway labourer, and Elizabeth Nash of Pratts Bottom, (buried 29th May).

1868, 4th April, Robert, son of Levi, railway labourer, and Elizabeth Foster of Pratts Bottom, received 12th January 1873.

1868, 12th April, Rosetta, daughter of Joseph, railway labourer, and Sarah Anne Bray of Pratts Bottom.

1868, 12th April, Sarah Elizabeth, daughter of the same above, aged 6.

Marriages

1865, 30th May, Henry Sayer, full age, bachelor, of Herne, publican, son of Thomas Sayer, coach proprietor:
    Elizabeth Lansbury, full age, spinster, daughter of James Lansbury, railway contractor, by licence. Witnesses, Thomas Lansbury, M. E. Lansbury.

1867, 11th May, Thomas Richard Read, 25, bachelor, railway labourer, son of Thomas Read, soldier:
    Hannah Stone, 21, spinster, daughter of Daniel Stone, labourer.
    Witnesses, John Pitchers, George Brooks (Parish Clerk).

Burials

John George Skeels, aged 4 months of the Railway Huts, buried July 24th 1864.

James Lansbury, aged 22 years of the Railway Huts, buried October 23rd 1864, killed by trucks running over him.

William Horne, (name uncertain), of the Railway Huts, aged about 45, buried October 23rd 1864, found dead in railway cutting, supposed to have fallen over.

William Copper, aged 5 years, probably son of railway worker of Well Hill, buried February 1865.

Emma Dodd, aged 3 years of the Railway Huts, buried April 29th 1865.

Alice Overton, aged 5 months of the Railway Huts, buried August 13th 1865.

Philip Townsend, aged 20 years of Chelsfield, buried 6th January 1866, crushed in Chelsfield Tunnel.

Robert Barclay, aged 5 months of the Railway Huts, buried May 25th 1866.

Henry Bray, aged 6 years of Pratts Bottom, scalded to death by accident, son of a railway worker.

John William Nash, aged 6 weeks of Chelsfield, buried May 29th 1867, son of a railway labourer.

William Clark, aged 27 years of the Railway Huts, Warren Lane, buried September 20th 1867.

Warren Road and New Chelsfield

A walk of about 1¾ miles

From the rear (west) of the Church a path runs beside the "new" part of the graveyard and across a field to Warren Road. Over to your left is Court Lodge Farm. Cross the road to find a footpath running parallel to it as does a strip of land and on the far side another footpath and bridle path. The strip of land was acquired by Kent County Council in the late 30's for a proposed Dartford crossing approach first proposed as early as 1927 as an east-west main thoroughfare and not finally abandoned until c1964, probably to the relief of everyone unconnected with the road building industry which was later compensated with the M25 contracts. The land is now a public amenity.

Warren Road

During the building of the railway Warren Road was the site of the railway huts although I can not tell you their exact location. Sites like these were everywhere during the railway building age. The huts were built with any materials available, local stone (there is sandstone in this area), mud, some brick and timber. Roofing would be tarpaulin, tiles or a mixture. There was usually a floor of stones or gravel so it did not get too muddy in wet weather, or at least that was the theory. Some of the huts would be occupied by families who would take as many lodgers as they could cram in. Others would be run by shanty keepers, charging rent and finding accommodation for new employees as they were taken on or as others left or died. 4d a night was the norm for a bed, 1d if they slept on a table and 1/2d for the floor. Wages were 17s to 18s per week c1868. Most were paid partly in cash (beer money) and partly in tokens which were to be exchanged in an employer owned shop where you could bet someone was getting a rake off. Amazingly this type of payment was made illegal in 1837 but still persisted into the 1860's. You would probably see evidence of drinking everywhere you looked, for the navvies were sold beer as they worked. It would have been a good deal safer than the water. In the huts wives were taken and children born; all lived in cramped and unsanitary conditions. Older children frequently ran off to try and find a better life.

The most hazardous work of all was tunnelling, working deep under ground, often soaked with muddy water, in constant peril from a collapse and breathing foul air. Shifts were 12 hours day and night and accidents were frequent.

After the opening of the railway manure was dispatched from London, where there was plenty of it, with an estimated 300,000 tons of horse manure produced a year in the 19th century in the Cities of London and Westminster alone (not in those days a low emission zone). It was unloaded into heaps at Chelsfield Station and then onto wagons to be taken for use on fields, quite a lot of it via Warren Road. This brought forth many complaints which continued right into the 20th century. At a Council meeting on 6th October 1908 a letter from the Rev J. J. Baddeley, Rector of Chelsfield, was referred to with reference to an alleged nuisance arising from refuse in trucks at Chelsfield Station and from the cartage there of. A report from the Sanitary Inspector stated that several contractors had at his request provided proper side boards to their carts. On the 8th December 1914 a complaint was mentioned from a lady in Warren Road of a nuisance from flies and gnats on her premises. The Medical Officer thought it advisable that further enquires be made as to the existence of quantities of flies at other houses in the neighbourhood with approximate distances of such houses from the railway station where a large quantity of manure is delivered and from the site of a large heap which was deposited near the road and had remained there a long time.

During the 1920's George Miller of Wested Farm, Crockenhill, became known as the "Peppermint King". He grew the plant, among other places in fields along Warren Road. By the time his son Albert took over in the 30's 420 acres of peppermint were under cultivation. The plant grows to about 20 inches (50cm) in late Summer with pinkish-mauve flowers. When harvested it was sent to Mitcham Distillery at Mill Green, run at that time by W. J. Bush. The mill was established in the 1840's by another George Miller (I can't say if there was any family connection) later becoming J & G Miller. It used water power from an eastern branch of the Wandle. Part of the mill site was still in use for peppermint processing until the early 1960's as Holland's Distillery, (who later relocated), but it has now gone. The Millers also grew lavender.

Continuing westwards along the path nearest the road you come opposite Court Lodge Farmhouse, built in 1863 to replace Court Lodge as the working centre of the farm. It is a rather plain square house with a small porch. There is also a small business park, the most predominant occupant being Chelsfield Motor Works who will undertake most work on most cars. Established in 1970 they claim to be the largest independent garage in the Orpington area. There is also a neat 19th century stable block occupied by Stem Florists.

Almost directly opposite alongside the bridle path at the other side of the strip is a stone memorial to R.A.F. Sergeant John Hugh Mortimer Ellis of 85 Squadron who died near this spot on 1st September 1940 in Hurricane P2673. He was 21 and "One of Churchill's Few". The memorial was placed here in 2006 by the Shoreham Aircraft museum, Shoreham village, at the time of writing open Sundays from May to September 10.00 a.m. to 5 p.m. Apparently some horse riders have complained that their mounts have been frightened by the stone.

Continuing down the bridle path or adjacent footpath you come to the Chelsfield Vista at a view point which looks towards Orpington and beyond to London and Docklands. The board indicates the landmarks that can be seen including Canary Wharf and Crystal Palace. This view site was created in 1994.

The paths terminate at the station car park at the end of The Highway. The view of Chelsfield Station from here has probably not changed a lot since 1868. The railway related structures have of course been updated from time to time and there may be a few less hedgerows but the overall scene can not be much different.

Continue down Warren Road past a pleasant looking close of modern houses called Knights Ridge and over the railway bridge. Just before the R1 bus stop a short path to the right goes though some trees and bushes to the fairly modern Russett Close which in turn leads to Warren Drive, a road of stock late 30's houses. We are now in New Chelsfield, This name was being used in the early 20th cent. when few homes existed here. The major development was began by Morrell Ltd from c1935. Go left then right into Warren Road. The left hand side starts with more 30's homes. Opposite 203 on a woodland area is an information board which will tell you that this is Chelsfield Green, a Bromley Council Nature Conservation Area. It has also been known as Spring Gardens but was originally Aspen Spring which gave its name to a pair of Waring estate cottages. These are the only pair of 1860's ones built to have now gone, the site now occupied by two large modern houses. There is no record of any spring ever being here but "spring" in this case refers to a wood. 181-183 Warren Road is a block of late 30's maisonettes with 3/4 rounded bays to each. Edwardian 177 looks to have been once a pair with a neighbour on its right where there is now a block of modern flats. 175 is probably also Edwardian.

Turn up Albert Road to Crown Road. There are some more Edwardian homes, 29 is dated 1911 and 21 has an interesting Tudor style extension to the rear right. 13 is a cottage of 1909 while 4 and 6 could be late Victorian, 6 probably starting as a pair. 5 is a large 20's or 30's detached. Modern Crown Close is on the corner with Edith Road. Going down here you find a turn of the century terrace on the left, 12A being a later addition, its brickwork not keyed in to its neighbour. The junction at Warren Road is flanked by probably late 19th century cottages, number 155 has later external timbering.

Although not all strictly within our area the lower end of Warren Road is of some interest. The centre has a wide wooded strip. The north side below 59 is mostly stock 30's houses with Warren Road School behind. First opened in 1938 the school was rebuilt between 1987 and 1989 in two phases (by the Borough Architect); the junior building having some attractive arched windows and porthole windows. The south side of Warren Road has some interesting mainly Edwardian and 20's houses between 8 and 66, the most notable being 8, "Warren House", on the corner of Warren Avenue, used by the school between 1944 and 1948 as additional accommodation and canteen, and number 42, in arts and crafts style has very unusual tall stone chimneys one of them roofed. The remainder of this side of Warren Road together with Warren Gardens and The Brackens is all modern.

Walk up Woodside which is again modern except for two older detached, and also here is a small very new Apostolic Church, all towards the top end. At the end of Goldfinch Close, about half way up Woodside, a wooded footpath leads to Green Street Green. This is another relic of the once proposed Dartford crossing approach. Kent County Council began negotiations with land owners to acquire a strip 120 feet wide in September 1937. To include cycle lanes it would have led to the Dartford-Purfleet tunnel.

Take the footpath opposite the close and keeping to the right you arrive at Windsor Drive adjacent to the Methodist Church. The foundation stone reads 19-11-66. Rather plain and practical architecturally but if open you can go in and see the small pane of glass from the kitchen at Hewitts etched with "16 Feb 1812", the date of the first Methodist meeting in Chelsfield village. It was damaged unfortunately during a burglary (some people have no shame), but has been reinstated to its proper place. The interior of the church is functional but quite welcoming with a nicely proportioned organ.

Next door is the Chelsfield centre also from the 1960's. Windsor Drive was a track-way until c1935 when Morrell began developing this area and it was at first just known as New Planning Road until early 1937 when it gained its present name. Morrell Estate and Development Co. Ltd. appear to have had financial problems leading to a liquidator being appointed by 1937 although they remained trading at least to finish the developments they had started. Two of the earliest buildings in the road are the bungalows at 145/147, one having an unusual rounded porch in the internal angle of its frontage. The other may have been similar but since altered. A short distance away on the opposite side of Windsor Drive is an entrance to Glentrammon Recreation Ground. Foxbury Drive and Daleside are modern houses similar to those fronting Windsor Drive. These were constructed from 1946 by Comonte & Co. who had taken over a large part of Morrell's site. Turn into High Beeches which together with The Retreat was the first part of the Morrell residential construction (more of their 30's bungalows feature). The actual High Beeches trees are behind the Retreat. The naming of the road High Beeches brought strong objections from the owner of a house called "High Beeches" who was worried about his post being mis-delivered and the road was very nearly renamed High Beeches Avenue.

On the evening of 20th October 1936 Amy Johnson nearly crashed here on what would have at that time been a construction site with maybe some homes completed. She was flying from Le Bourget to Croydon when reduced visibility forced her down. On her second attempt at landing in one of Morrell's fields next to Warren Road she thought the ground too rough and went round again. She was successful on her third attempt apart from the plane being upside down. The plane, a Beechcraft D17 single engined biplane with an enclosed cockpit, somersaulted onto its back. She had switched the engine off and undone her safety belt as she had a fear of being trapped. She suffered a fractured nose from hitting the windscreen and a dislocated shoulder. Pulled out of the plane by a lorry driver and other passing road users she was treated by Doctor J. Belcher at Morrell's site hut. An ambulance was called but was not required. After treatment she was driven home by a news reporter looking for a scoop but when they arrived the rest of the press were already there. She gave an interview from an armchair with her arm in a sling, a plaster on her nose and bloodspots in her hair. To make matters worse the majority of the questions were not about her accident but concerned her fading marriage.

Amy Johnson was born in Hull in 1903 and worked as a typist to finance her flying lessons, gaining her provisional licence in 1929. She became the first woman to fly solo from England to Australia in May 1930 winning the £10,000 prize offered the Daily Mail. In 1931 she flew to Japan via Moscow and in 1932 flew to Cape Town and back. She married Jim Mollison, a Scottish aviator in 1932 and they set several records together but divorced after six years. Amy's luck ran out in 1941, while in the Air Transport Auxiliary, she was delivering a new Airspeed Oxford when it got into difficulties. All that is known for certain is that both engines of the plane had stopped when it came down on the water near the East Knock John buoy in the Thames estuary. Witnesses and "experts" beg to differ on everything else. Her body was never recovered.

At the lower end of High Beeches turn back into Windsor Drive to reach the shops. The three storey block and the pair were completed by Morrell or their successors by 1938. The larger block shows a degree of ornamentation including tile panels as it was intended that the shopping area would develop. It did but only to the extent of six more plain two storey units. At the time of writing the shops include, a motor factors, two convenience stores, a pharmacy, a dentist, a glazier, a Post Office, a health food shop, a betting office, a hairdressers, a flooring specialist, a tanning and health centre, a kitchen/bathroom/bedroom specialist, an Indian restaurant, a veterinary clinic and if you now like Chelsfield so much you would like to live here I'm sure you would find the estate agents most helpful.

Up Meadway the Morrell development continues and just past Spring Gardens (laid out late 1936), the "join" with the Homesteads Chelsfield Park is obvious. Back at Windsor Drive The Chelsfield pub is also c1938 built for Cannons Brewery in typical 30's pub style. For a while it was called the Heavy Horse. We now arrive back where we started at Chelsfield Station. Why not go round again sometime?

Warren Road and New Chelsfield

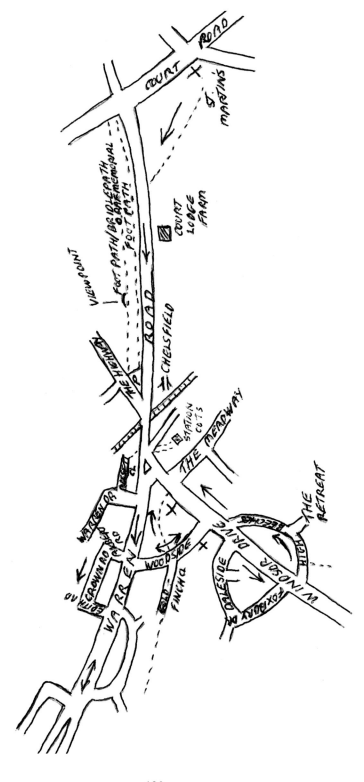

"Warren House", Warren Road.

An unusual chimney on a house in Warren Road.

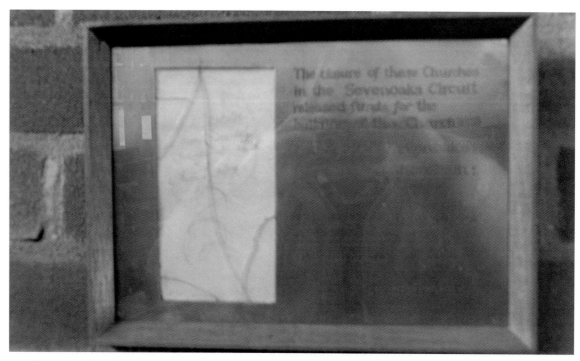

On the wall in the Methodist Church is the pane of glass from Hewitts. It was damaged during a burglary but has been reinstated.

The Methodist Church interior.

1930's bungalows in High Beeches.

The main shopping terrace, Windsor Drive.

KENTISH TIMES, FRIDAY, OCTOBER 23, 1936.

MRS. MOLLISON INJURED.

FORCED LANDING AT CHELSFIELD.

'Plane Overturns.

Mrs. Mollison sustained injury to her shoulder when the aeroplane in which she was flying alone from Paris to Croydon overturned after a forced landing near Chelsfield Village on Tuesday evening.

The famous airwoman was helped from the cabin of her machine by a lorry-driver who saw the accident.

Mrs. Mollison said that she was flying from Le Bourget to Croydon and had been given a favourable weather report. Over the Channel, off Dungeness, a fog developed and became so dense that she did not see the English coast until she was actually over it.

"ALMOST BLIND FLYING."

After half-an-hour of "almost blind flying," she began circling and looking for Croydon. Round and round she went in a radius of 10 miles, but could see no sign of the airport. She had noticed a useful-looking field marked by a white road, and as it was getting dark she decided to land there.

Twice she tried to come down on it. On the first attempt it looked as though she would run into the houses, so she zoomed upwards. On the second attempt she came in short, but the ground was so rough she had to keep going and make another attempt. This time she came in short again, and after landing put on the brakes to avoid running into the houses surrounding the field.

"EVERYTHING WENT TOPSY-TURVY."

"Then," Mrs. Mollison continued, "everything went topsy-turvy. As I put on the brakes I suppose my wheels hit a rut, because the aeroplane went right over on its back. I had already switched off the engine, but I had not time to turn off the petrol. I had undone my safety belt, as I have a horror of being trapped in an aeroplane if it crashes. If the belt had been done up I should probably not have smacked my nose on the dashboard. I think I must

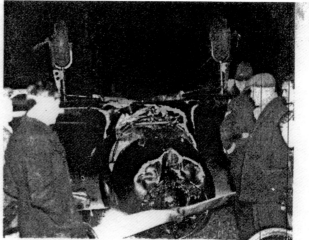

MRS. MOLLISON CRASHES AT CHELSFIELD.—The damaged plane lying upside down on the Goddington Estate, Chelsfield.

have turned a complete somersault in the cabin."

The landing place was one of Morrell's fields. Motor-cyclists and cyclists passing along the Orpington by-pass and Warren-road noticed the machine wobbling, and when it had landed they rushed to the spot. They found the 'plane turned over and in the cabin they could see a woman, whom they did not at first recognise as Mrs. Mollison. The glass of the cabin was smashed and Mrs. Mollison was dragged out in a dazed condition. Papers in the cabin revealed her identity.

Mrs. Mollison was taken to Morrell's Estate Office and Dr. J. Belcher was sent for. He found that she had facial injuries and was suffering from shock.

A NARROW ESCAPE.

Mrs. Mollison's clothing was soaked in petrol. Fortunately, before landing, she had stopped the engine. There were blood-stains on the machine, the undercarriage and nose of which were damaged.

The officials of Morrell's Estate did everything possible for Mrs. Mollison. An ambulance stood by from the County Hospital, Farnborough, but this was not required, as Mrs. Mollison was able to leave by car for her home in Kensington. Her nose in plaster was the only indication that she had had an accident.

Mrs. Mollison stated later that she intends to continue her flying career under her maiden name of Miss Amy Johnson.

Left: The story as it appeared in the local newspaper.

Next page: An artist's fanciful impression of Morrell's development at Chelsfield Station, including cinema. The map is not very accurate either, showing amongst other errors, St. Martin's on the wrong side of the bypass.

★ There are wonderful
Opportunities for EVERYBODY at
CHELSFIELD
KENT

Artist's impression of MORRELL'S Chelsfield Estate showing proposed development.

CHELSFIELD—Once a sleepy Railway Station is now the hub of a Garden Town growing with phenomenal rapidity.

Chelsfield has totally eclipsed any previous Garden Town Scheme ever known !

Chelsfield is on the Map !

Sweeping into popularity day by day. The time is opportune !

Seize it, to investigate the possibilities of Chelsfield from your view point. Whether your interest is **BUSINESS, BUILDING, INVESTING or SEEKING YOUR FUTURE HOME —SEE CHELSFIELD—SOON !**

A selection from Morrell's 61 types of Modern Homes is illustrated above.

1. Morrell's Type A.1. £1,295 freehold. 30 3 weekly
2. Morrell's Type 2. £625 freehold 14 6 weekly
3. Morrell's Type B.G. £825 freehold. 19 3 weekly
4. Morrell's Type K.I. £675 freehold. 15 9 weekly
5. Morrell's Type C.5. £745 freehold. 17 4 weekly

Chelsfield Station, which is in the centre of the Estate, is easily accessible from the seven termini of the Southern Electric Railway and intermediate stations. Journey time 30 minutes.

There are no Extras whatever—£1 secures.

Detached and Semi-detached Houses and Bungalows, Flats and Maisonettes, are here awaiting your inspection, with prices ranging from £575 freehold, 13/5 weekly, to £4,000. Show House open every day, including Sundays, until Dusk.

CHELSFIELD IS THE NEXT STATION TO ORPINGTON

FARES refunded to all visitors this week-end, travelling within 15 miles radius. Obtainable on request at the Estate Office in Warren Road, Chelsfield, outside Chelsfield Station. Chelsfield is served direct from New Cross, Lewisham, Chislehurst, and intermediate stations, or Herne Hill, Beckenham, Bromley South, and intermediate stations from Victoria.

Or write for free travelling vouchers (state number required) and booklet to Morrell (Builders) Ltd., Terminal House, Victoria, S.W.1. Phone: SLOane 7176

Name..

Address..

....

MORRELL'S CHELSFIELD ESTATE Kent

Aspen Spring in Warren Road, the only pair of of the Waring estate cottages to have gone, seen here more or less how they would have looked originally.

Further Reading

"Chelsfield Chronicles" by Geoffrey Copus. Has to be top of the list for anyone wanting more on the history of Chelsfield.

"Half-lights on Chelsfield Court Lodge" by Alexander Theodore Brown. Contains material on the Morland and Crawford families at Court Lodge and Brass Crosby.

"Millennial Halstead" by Geoffey Kitchener. A Kentish village story.

"A Woman of Passion The Life of E. Nesbit 1858-1924" by Julia Briggs. An in depth study of this writer's life and work.

"Early Days" by Miss Read. Childhood memories from Chelsfield and Hither Green.

"This Forgotten Place", **"And Then There Were None"** and **""Till The End of Time"** by Derek Sheffield. A trilogy based on his grandparents life at the hamlet of Maypole. While these books contain useful information about Chelsfield they also include stories of a personal nature concerning other residents of the area which are best treated with a degree of caution.

"The Story of Green Street Green" by Marjorie Ford and Geoffrey Rickard.

"Pratts Bottom an English Village" by Judith Hook.

"Pratts Bottom A Journey Through Life" by Sue Short. A larger and more recent publication than the above with information on Chelsfield Park.

"Kent", A Barracuda Guide to County History Vol. 1 by T. A. Bushell. A day by day history of Kent, easy to follow.

"Martin of Tours, Parish Priest, Mystic and Exorcist" by Christopher Donaldson. The life and work of the Saint.

"Chelsfield Park Residents Association Millennium booklet, 2001" edited by Paul Vinton. A short history of the estate.

"Warren Road Primary School 1938 - 1998" by Janice English. The first sixty years.

"Asprey 1781 - 1981" by Bevis Hillier. A family history.

"A History of Knockholt In The County of Kent" by David Waldron Smithers. The village the station was named after.

"Orpington to Tonbridge" Southern main lines series by Vic Mithchell and Keith Smith. Has useful illustrations of Chelsfield and Knockholt stations.

"Down the Line To Hastings" by Brain Jewell. Less detailed than the above but includes the whole main line.

"Railways to Sevenoaks" by Charles Devereux. A history.